AFRICA IN TIME-PERSPECTIVE

Marta

AFRICA IN

TIME-PERSPECTIVE

A DISCUSSION OF HISTORICAL RECONSTRUCTION
FROM UNWRITTEN SOURCES

By DANIEL F. McCALL

New York
OXFORD UNIVERSITY PRESS
1969

First published by
Boston University Press, Boston, 1964,
and
Ghana University Press, Legon, 1964

Paperback edition,
Oxford University Press, New York, 1969

Printed in the United States of America

PREFACE TO
THE PAPERBACK EDITION

The response to the original edition of *Africa in Time-Perspective* has been very gratifying. I have been informed by teachers in a number of universities that they have put it on a syllabus either as required or as recommended reading. In order to make it more readily available to students and in an inexpensive form, this paperback edition has been prepared. The text has not been reworked, but a brief bibliographical essay covering relevant works which have appeared in the last half decade has been appended.

Since the proof of the pudding is in the eating, it might be appropriate to announce that since the completion of this work in late 1962, I have been intermittently engaged in research using certain of these methods and have been attempting to bring together and synthesize my results with the findings of others to achieve a history of Africa from the beginning of the Neolithic to the advent of Islam. It will take at least two more years before it will be completed.

Wollaston Hill   D. F. McCALL
January 1969

PREFACE

THIS series of lectures came about through the suggestion of Professor John D. Fage, then professor of history at the University College of Ghana, and the approval of the idea by his successor, Professor Graham Irwin, which led to an invitation from the Principal, R. H. Stoughton, to me to give some Open Lectures during the academic year 1960–1961.

An informal exchange from the African Studies Program, Boston University, made possible my acceptance of this invitation. It was possible for me to formulate somewhat more fully a number of ideas that I had been developing in classroom discussion for four or five years.

My first reaction was that it was an opportunity to do something I wanted very much to do, and I thought of it then in more grandiose terms than my subsequent efforts have accomplished; but the delimitation has been deliberate and for several reasons. In the flush of early enthusiasm, I had visualized this eventual volume as a handbook which could provide the neophyte with an adequate guide to the use of all the techniques of research in these varied and confusing fields of historical research. Certainly, we need such a book. This hope was premature for several reasons. (1) Some of the topics, e.g. archaeology, already have adequate handbooks which are in greater amplitude than could be squeezed into a book that has to cover so many other topics; and some studies, e.g. African art history, have clearly a long way to go before we can hope for an adequate handbook. (2) Lectures are more effective for description, exploration and inspiration than for instruction in technique; a handbook cannot result from a series of lectures, but only from, perhaps more tedious, laboratory-type demonstrations. And finally, my experience and my knowledge are not adequate to the task; it is, probably, not to be expected from a single individual, but may more likely result from a co-operative effort.

It is certainly to be hoped that such co-operative efforts will be directed to this end: the perfection of methodology. I hope that a series of conferences may be convened on the subject matter of this book, at least one for each chapter and perhaps a few others in areas where I have been neglectful. Then we may hope that handbooks will be produced, and though some will lag behind others, eventually we will find masters for all historical types of material, and even those who can integrate its great variety.

In view of the diversity of things discussed in this book, readers may wish to know something about the background of the author; it is a normal part of critical evaluation of a book to judge it in relation to the author's experiences and biases. The latter are usually harder to determine and often not less so for the author himself, but it is easy enough to recount the former. I went to Columbia University with a Bachelor's degree in history, but I studied anthropology there. A B.A. does not make one an historian, but it is at least an indication of an historical leaning, and my interests were such as to make me sensitive to the historical aspects of anthropology in my studies.

Some persons who know the steps in my career after leaving Columbia may be surprised to learn that history is such an old preoccupation of mine, for I turned at first to a study of urbanization (a topic in which I am still keenly interested). Many people would think that I was oriented to the present rather than the past, and that my rapprochement to sociology on the one hand excluded any concern with history. But there are common factors: sociology and history ought not to be such strangers as they often are in our university departments, and for me the study of urbanization, in as much as it was an aspect of social change, was an historic process, and I immersed myself in the history of urbanization as well as the current phenomena.

Most of the kinds of evidence, and the problems involved therein, discussed in this book would be considered by American scholars as properly in my field as an anthropologist. It is pertinent at this point to note that in different countries anthro-

pology has a varying scope. In the United States, the student of
anthropology must study four fields which together make up
the discipline: (1) social and cultural anthropology*; (2)
physical anthropology or human biology; (3) linguistics; (4)
archaeology. The student chooses one as his major emphasis
(I am a cultural anthropologist) and the other three together
are his minor. This means that he is not expected to be equally
competent in all fields, which would be perhaps an unrealizable
ideal. Even Franz Boas, who more than anyone is responsible
for establishing our American system of anthropological studies,
worked extensively in three fields, but did very little in archaeology. In Germany, *Anthropologie* and *Völkerkunde* are separate
academic entities, as in France are *Anthropologie* and *Ethnologie*.
Human Geography, which is more securely established in these
universities than in English-speaking countries, overlaps what
Boas delimited as anthropology. But the English-speaking
countries are not uniform: social anthropology as developed in
British universities since the advent of Bronislav Malinowski is
quite separate from linguistics, archaeology and physical
anthropology. It is therefore clear that I speak not only as an
anthropologist but as an American anthropologist; I do not
make the distinction invidiously but merely because it is pertinent to the content of the discussion. It is to my mind a pity that
there continue to be rather wide differences between the
national schools of anthropology, and it is encouraging to see
that closer common understandings are being achieved. Perhaps the division goes even deeper than just within anthropology: Radcliffe-Brown suggested that our goal should be a
unified social science. This may or may not be possible but, if it
is, a healing of the rift in anthropology would be a step in that
direction.

It may be relevant, too, that my earlier interest in history has
largely been in its 'exotic' branches: Asia and antiquity. There
may be more parallels to Africa in these fields than in modern
Europe and the United States.

The plan of the lectures has been maintained in the book,

---

* These two in themselves are rather different and some would oppose them and
pit one against the other; this is puerile. I follow my late, revered teacher, A. L.
Kroeber, in this: he said society and culture are like the two sides of a piece of
carbon paper; they are different, but do not function independently, and are
best considered together.

although it was cogently suggested that I move the chapter on Process so that it would follow the discussion of Evidence. I also felt inclined, while revising, to place the chapter on Ethnology to the end because it must deal with synthesizing various kinds of data, but it seemed best to follow the original outline.

The first chapter deals with the nature and admissibility of historical evidence; the second with archaeology; the third with oral traditions; the fourth with linguistics; the fifth with ethnology; the sixth with ethno-botany, ethno-zoology, human biology and epidemiology; the seventh with art; the eighth with chronology; the ninth with process; and the tenth with organization of research.

The audience for these lectures was mainly history students and teachers, but with an ample sprinkling of anthropologists. At certain points one group may have found the going more difficult for them than for the rest of the audience. If the focus has not been wholly consistent in terms of the academic division between the disciplines, it is unified at least in the pragmatic sense that those who write or study history, whatever their training, are historians.

To guard against the most grievous results of my own short-comings, I requested criticisms from a number of specialists on particular chapters. Many changes have been made as a result, but as one cannot keep up an endless dialogue, my critics have not seen the final draft before it went to press, and, in any case, of course, are not responsible for whatever errors may remain.

Professors William O. Brown, John D. Fage and Graham Irwin, having made possible the lectures, also read the manuscript.

A number of anthropologists were kind enough to give me comments. Professor Daryll Forde was generous enough to take time during the busy period of the Seminar on Ethno-History at Dakar to look over my work and to give me encouragement. Professors Joseph Greenberg, Elizabeth Colson, Philip Gulliver, and Simon Ottenburg gave me helpful suggestions on various parts of the book.

Professors Robert Moody, Frank Nowak and Dr. Norman Bennett of the History Department, and Jeffrey Butler of the African Studies Program of Boston University, and Professor Philip Curtin of Wisconsin gave me valuable comments.

William Fagg of the British Museum aided me in improving the chapter on art.

F. R. Irvine and Marvin Miracle pointed out some errors in the first formulation of the ethno-botany section.

I am most grateful to all of them for their help.

Boston, Mass.   DANIEL F. McCALL
March, 1962

CONTENTS

INTRODUCTION

THE probing by Man, by the sheer forces of his intellect, into the nature of things, himself included, is his unending preoccupation and distinguishing characteristic. The infinitesimal spaces of the atom and the infinite wastes of galactial space are both coming under surveillance. The time-axis as well as the space-axis is being explored. The future is being anticipated by the study of trends and planning for various phases of society; the past is being recovered by a growing battery of relatively new and continually improving techniques.

The practical aspects of investigating the physical structure and functioning of the universe are obvious and have already catapulted the amenities of everyday life for millions of people beyond the means of even the kings and emperors of previous times. The attempts to anticipate and plan for the future, if not actually to prophesy, are also, although sometimes suspect, generally welcomed. But of what use is a knowledge of the past? Let the dead bury the dead, is the attitude of the pragmatic man.

Attempts to 'use' history have usually involved distorting it, either blatantly or mildly, by a political party, church, imperialist nation, or interest group of some kind. A few have set out to 'use' history, on the other hand, in a way which depended on the accuracy of the historical analysis: this is the attempt to draw lessons for the present from the past. This has been seldom done seriously and even more seldom have such studies been accepted by either officials or scholars; the objections are that history does not repeat itself (despite the fact that events from different periods and places may fall into the same class of events—from which some generalizations may tentatively be drawn); and the number of variables is so great (i.e. the societies are in many ways so different) that it is not possible to make adequate allowance for them. Eventually perhaps historical sociology may help to bring greater control over the variables and make possible safer generalizing.

Some historians prefer therefore not to claim any usefulness for history, but to see it as a cultural or aesthetic undertaking like the creation and appreciation of art; a fulfilment of some indefinable psychological or temperamental yearning for satisfaction, but something that can be done without—it is, one might infer, a luxury.

Others make a case for history as a necessary part of a civilized society. It gives a humane and intellectual stature to an educated man with which his other studies cannot wholly supply him. Samuel Johnson said, 'Whatever makes the past, the distant, or the future predominate over the present, advances us in the dignity of thinking beings.' History is not alone in being able to achieve the effect that Dr. Johnson thought so laudable, but it, perhaps, does it more consistently than other studies. Without such people, who put the present in perspective, and perhaps without a predominance of such people, we may not be able to continue to survive in our dangerous nuclear age.

The world certainly needs leaders, and followers too, of great breadth of vision. History, especially a universal history, can help to construct this wide horizon of knowledge and understanding, but at this moment in time—one might say at this crisis—our existing histories are provincial and incomplete. This is not to deny that there have been monumental studies, but they do not yet add up to meet the needs of our time. Diodorus Siculus realized that the Roman Empire needed a history to reflect, define, and coalesce the new heterogeneous community that had been created, and he tried, perhaps unsuccessfully, to provide it in his prodigious work.

The task we face today is a far more herculean one, for our universe is not an empire but humanity and the globe. The accomplishment of this work cannot be the work of one man; it will have to be the synthesis of many men of many nations and many generations, but it is urgent that we get on with it as expeditiously as possible. In this book, I have tried to consider some of the problems implicit in any attempt to discover the history of Africa, a part of universal history which is still largely unwritten.

'Discover' is the right word. James T. Shotwell and Ernest F. Jacob wrote that 'This is the most remarkable chapter in the whole history of history—the recovery of that past which had already been lost when our literary history began.' Notable successes have been obtained in Crete and Peru; we must extend our efforts into other regions. The challenge in Africa is beginning to be met.

It has been asserted by Harry Elmer Barnes that the distinction between history and prehistory is no longer valid. 'Now,' he writes, 'when archaeology tells one much more of certain phases of the early life of man than was once known of even more recent periods through literary evidence, it is no longer accurate or logical to use the term "prehistoric", unless it is employed to designate that vague and hypothetical period in the beginnings of human development of which there exists no positive and tangible record, or unless one is limiting his conception to history as a branch of literature.' For myself, I am not for a moment content to agree that history should be limited to a branch of literature. Historical writing is literature, and often fine literature, but it is distinguished from most other forms of literary composition by the manner in which it is constructed, and—this is the more important point—in its functions, which I shall come back to in a moment. On the question of terminology, however, it does not seem to be, as Barnes claims, that 'prehistoric' is a 'now generally discredited term'. Many of those historians who continue to confine themselves to the use of written materials, as of course they are justified in doing if they so choose, have a tendency to use the term; and so do archaeologists. In fact, one of the disadvantages of the term is that archaeologists have practically appropriated it so that in some circles it is now virtually synonymous with archaeology. There is value in keeping history as the general term, that is, using it to include both; but we need a term that would denote that kind of history that is not based on written records. The distinction is logical because the techniques, and the training for them, are different, and therefore, despite some overlapping, the personnel concerned with them will tend to be different—

at least for some time to come. Barnes suggests the term 'pre-literary history' and this is an improvement on current usage, but it is a somewhat awkward term. I have always liked the term 'culture history', but that too is now encrusted with limiting connotations. Until a better designation can be found, I propose to use Barnes' suggestions.

One of the functions of history, some writers claim (and I agree with them) is to help the individual to define his personality: to see himself in the stream of humanity. For a nation, as well, it helps to indicate its character and its place in the world community. If this is true, and if it is also true that the world cannot longer remain half free and half unfree, then it can no longer continue half historic and half ahistoric.

The need for history can take aberrant forms, and in the name of providing history some persons may rather be creating myths. It can be argued that there is a need for myths, and if so, there is no harm so long as myth and history are not confused. There are ways of distinguishing the two. Stories like that of George Washington and the cherry tree, or of William Tell shooting an apple from his son's head never did any harm and are soon put in their proper category; but some myths can be dangerous, as we have recently seen in the case of the so-called *Myth of the Twentieth Century*. The best antidote to myth is better—and more—history. We need not worry too much then about a little myth-making, so long as historical research is making progress and educational systems make possible the dissemination of all varieties of history.

Although no one, these days, seems prepared to defend in print the maintenance of narrow boundaries for history, still in conversation with individual historians, objections sometimes are raised against the expansion of history into the non-literate period, because it requires so many kinds of skills. Can it be adequately and reliably done? We have enough instances now to say that it can; perhaps not often by a single person but as a cumulation of the efforts of many scholars. The discomfort of the objectors probably comes from the fact that the cultivation of this kind of history runs counter to the academic trend of recent decades to specialize. Whitehead and others have pointed out the dangers as well as the advantages in specialization; we must have generalizers as well. When the generalizer ventures in where the specialist fears to tread, he may be called a fool for his pains. This is an occupational hazard.

Leibnitz is called the last Renaissance man, in that since his time no one has been able to master all fields of knowledge. The Renaissance ideal is no longer possible because of the increase of knowledge, but the ideal has not for that reason become despicable. Our problem is to find a way to generalize from widely variant kinds of material, through committee, as it were, since it has become impossible for the individual.

If you radically change the size you affect the function; if you wish to continue to function to the same end with the different size, some modification of organization is necessary, for as Haldane* has shown, size and function are inextricably interwoven. When Rome outgrew the *polis* organization, the classical type of democracy failed to make an adjustment. Much later the idea of representation made possible a rebirth of democracy in a large state (I am not saying it brought about the rebirth, but only that it made it functionally possible.) The adjustment needed today in some areas of study is of analogous kind: a representation of disciplines in a generalizing parliament, metaphorically speaking.

These essays are not the beginning of the process and they certainly will not be the end. History, as Marc Bloch has so aptly written,

is an endeavour toward better understanding and, consequently, a thing in movement. To limit oneself to describing a science as it is will always be to betray it a little. It is still more important to tell how it expects to improve itself in the course of time. Now, such an undertaking inevitably involves a rather large dose of personal opinion. Indeed, every science is continually beset at every stage of its development by diverging tendencies, and it is scarcely possible to decide which is now dominant without prophesying the future.

I have tried not to betray history and I make no apology for my own opinion, but I set forth my vision of what historiography is becoming.

Boston, 1961

---

* 'On the Importance of Being the Right Size'.

The historian can rediscover what has been completely forgotten, in the sense that no statement of it has reached him by an unbroken tradition from eyewitnesses. He can even discover what, until he discovered it, no one ever knew to have happened at all. This he does partly by the critical treatment of statements contained in his sources, partly by the use of what are called unwritten sources, which are increasingly employed as history becomes increasingly sure of its own proper methods and its own proper criterion.

R. G. COLLINGWOOD

> I found that the historical evidence was more beautiful and . . .
> more interesting than all romantic fiction.
>
> *Leopold von Ranke*

CHAPTER ONE

WHAT IS HISTORICAL EVIDENCE?

HISTORY from unwritten sources may seem to many to be somewhat of an anomaly. History, it has generally been accepted, within the discipline itself, is based on documents. We shall have to look at these two words, *history* and *documents*, and see the various connotations in which they may be used.

This is to risk being fatuous and asking 'What is history?' But a great teacher of history has said, 'We all know what history is, until we ask, and then no one knows.' Many classroom discussions, I suppose, have started with the elimination of the layman's opinion that history is what has happened. It can only be, of course, what has been recorded of what happened.

There has to be a synthesis and interpretation of all pertinent records, of whatever kind they may be. This is the essence of the saying that heroes and conquerors do not make history; historians do. The closest the conqueror can come to *making* history is to be his own chronicler, as Julius Caesar was. This is perhaps why modern generals are so prolific with their memoirs. But still the historian has the last word, for he will take the various memoirs and much other material besides, edit them, and produce a synthesis that is constructed on some uniting thread of interpretation that he has selected.

Interpretation is an inescapable and indispensable aspect of history. Interpretation is not wholly, but largely, a subjective process. It depends on a personal selection of what is relevant in the search for inter-relationships between various classes of data. There is also a difference between historians on what is

emphasized as the unifying factors, common denominators, or grand themes of an historic period. That is why it is considered presumptuous to entitle a work *The History of* such and such because there can never be *The History*—there will be as many histories as historians. Yet there is not chaos. In time, and for a time, there develops a consensus among the authorities, but any settled question can be reopened, any consensus shattered, by new data, by a new methodological approach, or even sometimes by sheer ratiocination, and no historical epoch is closed— while historians are alive. Everything is subject to reinterpretation; there is no *final* historical truth.

Judgement and discretion are necessary to the historian, not only in interpreting his material but also in deciding what it is pertinent to include. All would agree that certain matters are relevant to the history of a given event or epoch, but beyond these there are usually many other matters that some historians will ignore and others will emphasize. This is constantly becoming a more complicated and difficult decision to make, and this is central to our discussion.

History, in the nineteenth century, but more particularly in the last few decades, has proliferated its interests into nearly every field of human activity. We now speak of social history, economic history, intellectual history, the history of medicine, of science, of literature and so on. Each of these new areas of inquiry demanded new skills on the part of the historian. We now expect that the social historian will be acquainted with sociology as well as history; that the economic historian will have more than a modicum of economics. In other words, the direction of an historian's interest determines the extra-historical skills that he must have. The lines between the two fields, though not erased, are successfully bridged. It may be, sometimes, that a practitioner of one of the other fields ventures into history, as in the case of Hans Zinsser,[1] who gave us histories of certain diseases that have afflicted man.

Historians of Africa can pursue these now-established sub-branches of history. The social, economic, medical and intellectual history of this continent or parts thereof, is beginning to emerge from research recently done or in progress, and this is in fact one of the most stimulating developments of recent years to both historians and Africanists. African history is a field that is just opening up and many questions demand our attention. It is this challenge which is so attractive to young scholars, and that has been responsible for the recent surge of discussion and research.

But in Africa there is a further challenge, which, while not non-existent elsewhere, is less felt in countries where there is something approaching a surfeit of written documents. This generation of African historians has the opportunity of pioneering in the use of unwritten sources as not so long ago social and economic historians and others pioneered a number of new sub-branches of history. I am not suggesting that this has not been attempted in earlier generations. There have been forerunners and some significant ones, but they have failed to establish the field or to perfect the methodology.

Let us come back now to the words *history* and *documents*. We must never mistake etymology for definition, but the derivation of a word tells us something of what the original concept was in its emphasis and delimitations and is of importance in understanding the changing connotations that the word has had in different periods during which it has been in use.

The word 'ἱστορία meant simply 'inquiry'. Herodotus worked less with written chronicles than by inquiring of persons who had information of local events in their own times and the times of their predecessors. The oldest written history now extant, that was composed by a West African, the *Tarikh el-Fettech*, uses virtually the same idiom in its title, *The Chronicle of the Searcher*, and Mahmoud Kâti went about his task in essentially the same way that Herodotus did.

Even in the beginning the meaning *inquiry* was restricted by the emergent historians. In essence, as broad in scope as its more modern and prestigious synonym, *research*, 'ἱστορία was limited to inquiry into the affairs of men and women in societies; but, by convention, it became even more limited, and in practice was generally restricted to the dynastic, political and military, and sometimes religious activities, and to a large extent thus it remained until only about a century ago. The manifold expansion in the scope of activities which historians have now come to accept as pertinent to history have not, however, in general caused them to depart from an almost total dependence upon written sources. Geology and astronomy

share with history the characteristic of having a time dimension
—and we might note that they perceive the past without written
sources.

What is meant by the word, document? In the historical
profession, not long ago, this would have been taken to mean
a piece of writing. To say a 'written document' would have been
a tautology; to say a 'non-written document' would have been
a self-contradiction. But the word is now used in a wider sense
by historians, and in popular usage the connotations can be
quite varied. The word can be used as a synonym of *record*, for
instance, to say that the fossil imprint of a dinosaur's foot is a
record of its former existence in the locality. Archaeological
artifacts are spoken of as *records* of the past. Voices or other
sounds on tape or wax are records or recordings. French
ethnologists call oral traditions, 'la documentation orale'. We
speak of a certain kind of serious film as a 'documentary film'.
One can go so far as to include in the term *documents* all kinds of
data, however preserved, and historians today see nothing
revolutionary in such a designation, but in practice few have
used unwritten documents extensively.

The acceptance by historians of unwritten sources as a
possibility coupled with a neglect of them in practice is illustrated by Louis Gottschalk in his essay 'The Historian and the
Historical Document'. In the opening section under the
heading *Definitions*, he writes:

The word document has been used by historians in several senses.
On the one hand, it is sometimes used to mean any written source
of historical information as contrasted with oral testimony or with
artifacts, pictorial survivals and archeological remains.[2]

This is, of course, the older use of the word which continues to
have some currency in the profession. Gottschalk continues:

On the other, it is sometimes reserved for only official and state
papers such as treaties, laws, grants, deeds, etc.[3]

The phrasing is misleading in the above because this second
usage is not the opposite of the distinction made in the first
instance, it is merely a special case of the first usage, i.e. some
historians working on certain problems found it convenient to
limit the use of *document* to refer to a selected range of written

sources. As his third and final example of how the word is used, Gottschalk gives us the more inclusive sense which has become accepted in modern historiography.

Still another sense is contained in the word *documentation*, which, as used by the historian *inter alios*, signifies any process of proof based upon any kind of source whether written, oral, pictorial or archeological. For the sake of clarity, it seems best to employ the word *document* in the last, most comprehensive definition, which is etymologically correct, using *written documents* and *official documents* to designate the less comprehensive categories. Thus *document* becomes synonymous with *source*.[4]

Under the rubric *Sources*, he had already mentioned 'archaeological' and 'numismatical' materials. One can conclude from this that the newer usage has triumphed and that the word *document* unless qualified by a limiting adjective is to be understood as including unwritten sources. This decision is in keeping with the principles of lexicography as it brings under a single term all the things which may be used for the same purpose. Indeed, it may have been in large part an inclination to lexical tidiness that has determined the decision to accept the comprehensive definition as the standard one. It is safer to have a general term to use, and avoid being charged with overlooking something that is pertinent to the topic; it can then always be claimed that the unspecified item is implicit in the general term, and of course one cannot specify everything.

At any rate, in the next section, headed *Types of Documents*, Gottschalk proceeds to discuss *only* written sources! Type VII, 'Fiction, Song, Poetry and Folklore', could easily include oral literature (and perhaps was intended to do so) but the discussion is confined to Chaucer and other written literature. No 'type of document' is listed that would include 'artifacts, pictorial survivals and archeological remains'. Now that he has got down to business, the author seems to have forgotten the platitudes which he felt it was necessary to make in the introduction.

In later sections, Gottschalk discusses external and internal criticism of documents. Although many points could apply to oral sources, we cannot doubt that he had written sources mainly in mind, and there is no discussion of problems of evaluation of 'pictorial survivals', or 'numismatical materials' which he had mentioned earlier. The only direction given, which is hardly explicit, is not in the sections on criticism but is to be found back in the introductory section of *Definitions*, where we are informed that for archaeological and numismatical materials the historian 'has to depend largely upon museums'.

Gottschalk's work is used in many universities as a standard reference and is thus important in the formation of students' conception of *document*. Yet it is apparent that Gottschalk has merely recognized unwritten sources as some sort of shibboleth to which he must bow before getting down to what he considers is *really* pertinent.

The curious situation we find ourselves in is one in which the point of view that unwritten sources should be used by historians is *neither* revolutionary *nor* established. In the last half century in particular, the point of view has become familiar but it has not been fully applied.

Where are these unwritten documents to be obtained? They are produced by the disciplines of archaeology, linguistics, ethnology, ethno-botany, and ethno-zoology, physical anthropology and serology, geography, physics and the analysis of art. The historian can, in fact, treat some of this data as simply another written source by taking the books, articles, monographs and reports of the workers in these fields, but he may also, if he is daring, venture into these fields himself, after some preparation, and obtain primary material from his own investigations. The first possibility has been explored; the second continues to be neglected. We will come back to this.

Utilizing the writings of social scientists was for a while graced by the designation, the 'New History'. Historians have long since become used to—one might say inured to—hearing about the 'New History'. James Harvey Robinson hailed it as early as 1913. Robinson proclaimed:

The 'New History' is escaping from the limitations formerly imposed on a study of the past. . . . it will avail itself of all those discoveries that are being made about mankind by anthropologists, economists, psychologists and sociologists.[5]

Valiant onslaughts were made on these 'limitations that were formerly imposed on a study of the past'. Certainly Charles Beard, for one, availed himself of the discoveries of the economists, and he has given us, as a result, among other studies, a non-Marxist economic interpretation of the American Constitution.[6] A. Duggan, for another, has utilized the discoveries of the psychologists and has essayed to exhibit for us the thoughts that passed through the mind of Henry II.[7] The discoveries of sociology are so well integrated into history that it has recently been said that there is no further use for the term social history, as this cannot be separated from other types of history. But where is the contribution of anthropology?

Anthropology was listed first by Robinson but presumably only because the order was alphabetical. Despite the influence which Sir James Frazer and a few other anthropologists have had on the thinking of some historians, there is not a school of historians that could be called anthropological, as there are schools of economic, psychological and social historians. Perhaps this can be explained as a result of the fact that anthropology only recently turned its attention to literate societies and history is just beginning to consider non-literate societies.

Economics, psychology and sociology have been concerned, as history (to a somewhat lesser extent) has also, *almost* exclusively with western societies. The data gained by each field fitted with the other because they each studied variant aspects of the same entity. Anthropology could have contributed more than it did but most anthropologists were studying other cultures—cultures in which historians in general had not yet become interested. Now that both anthropologists and historians have broadened their view there is more opportunity—and necessity—for an interchange.

To the extent that historians of occidental countries borrow from the recent studies by anthropologists of western culture, the interchange between anthropology and history is on the now-familiar pattern of rapprochement between history and the social sciences and is perhaps the completion of the programme outlined by Robinson. The historians will already have utilized the information provided by sociologists on western institutions and will have interpreted the personalities in the light of psychologists' findings of their cases and samples taken in western countries, so that the anthropologists' contribution will, in general, be limited to an elucidation of the ethos, or value systems, of European and American societies.

When the historian, on the other hand, undertakes to write a history of an African society, the potential contribution of anthropology is far greater. Anthropology has specialized in the study of non-western societies, and the concept of 'culture' which is basic to this study has become by now thoroughly familiar to other disciplines where it is frequently referred to but often only indifferently used. To the extent that economists, sociologists, or psychologists have studied these other societies or individuals therein they will have become immersed to some extent in anthropology because their venture is cross-cultural. In large measure, however, it is the anthropologists themselves who will furnish the data on the structure of the society, the economy, institutions, the inventory of material culture (i.e. its goods and technology), the patterns of social change, and personality-norms of the African societies. All these aspects of social life are within the purview of anthropology. The historian will find himself in much more frequent contact with the anthropologist not only because of the latter's 'holistic' approach to society, but also because he is likely to be the only social scientist on the ground; other social scientists have been disinclined to study African societies, at least until very recently when a change of attitude has become noticeable.

All of the varied means of obtaining historical evidence which are discussed in the following chapters are branches of anthropology (or, in the case of physics, which provides the basis of chronology in certain instances, the co-operative relationship has already been worked out by anthropologists).

The number of points of contact between anthropology and history would seem to be considerably greater than in the case of the other social sciences. The other social sciences delimited their investigations to a segment of phenomena in complex societies (originally western but no longer necessarily so) whereas anthropology began as the study of simpler societies. It was therefore able to cover the whole range of social sciences, and even the humanities of the societies studied. But anthropology, benefiting from the development of the other social sciences, absorbed concepts and techniques and was encouraged to study more complex societies. Except for a few industrialized Asian nations which have trained their own sociologists, and psychologists, anthropology remains to a large extent the reservoir of social science information on non-western countries.

History, since the expansion of its interest into a wider range of social activities, is roughly parallel in scope to anthropology, but until recently the main focus of history was the West and the main focus of anthropology was elsewhere. The surge of interest by historians in non-western areas makes inevitable closer relationships than existed in the past between the two disciplines.

This favourable position for co-operation is not as yet generally perceived by either side but the arranging of these lectures on the initiative of the History Department at Legon is an indication that some historians are anxious to explore the means of liaison and the Marrett Lecture given by Evans Pritchard (to which we will return later) is an earnest that some anthropologists are thinking along similar lines.

At the moment, however, we still find in print statements which assert distinctions between the two which are misleading. These are generally written by anthropologists, as historians do not usually indulge in the exercise that seems endemic in the social sciences of contrasting their field with related studies. Even if the statements were true when written, many of them have been reprinted, quoted and passed on until they no longer reflect the present state of either discipline, and to be honest, most of the assertions needed more qualification even when originally written.

It is claimed that anthropology has a 'holistic' approach and concerns itself with all aspects of the life of a community and that it is therefore different from history, which is only 'past politics' or at the most 'the biography of states'. Some anthropologists seem to be unaware that there have been produced for Western Civilization or at least for constituent parts thereof, histories of law, land tenure, medicine, costume, cosmetics, art, technology, religion, commerce, ideas, language, attitudes towards pets and animals, morality, peasants, burgers, élites, the military, navies, literature, chastity belts, printing, institutions, games, ploughs, and windmills. In sum, what could be more holistic?

We are told that history is interested in the particular and the unique, whereas anthropology is concerned with the making of generalizations. The anthropologists who believed this did less than justice to history and ignored completely the philosophy of history. Certainly, Vico, Spengler and Toynbee have made as broad generalizations as Morgan, Tyler or Kroeber and have been as criticized for their pains.

It has been asserted that history was interested only in European civilization, its antecedents, its expansion and its contacts but not in the 'exotic' peoples themselves. While Europo-centric studies continue to form the bulk of historical writing, China, India, Japan, Korea, Persia and other countries have been studied by Western historians, and local historians, where they existed, have been thereby revivified, and where they did not previously exist they have come into being.

It was believed that history was properly concerned with literate peoples and that non-literate peoples would have to be left to anthropology and other disciplines. Nevertheless, the Scythians, Huns, Celts, Finns, Balts, Iberians, Etruscans and other peoples who had no writing (or left no corpus of inscriptions of sufficient size to be useful) have found their historians.[8]

The statements that neophyte anthropologists are apt to read about what constitutes history and perhaps the statements that neophyte historians are apt to read about what constitutes anthropology are usually outmoded. It is true that the main body of the membership of each profession remains distinguishable in interests from the other, and the average piece of research continues to reflect long-established concentrations; but the disciplines as a whole have more and more overlapped the scope of the other: in their recent extensions they nearly duplicate each other.

Yet even if anthropology enters into as intimate co-operation with history as the other social sciences have done, this will not necessarily bring historians into personal contact with unwritten sources.

The proponents of the 'New History' were not greatly concerned with unwritten sources, as such, but generally assumed that it would be sufficient to draw upon the writings of social scientists who might have used unwritten sources. The consequence of this limited view is that the concepts and some of the data of the social sciences have been incorporated into historical writing, but the methodology of the social sciences has not been used in historical research.

The purpose of this book is to suggest precisely that, in the research-design of historical investigation, primary considera-tion be given to the possibility of accumulating data by the means of anthropology. That is to say that the historian should not wait for the anthropologist to turn up a datum he can use, but that the arsenal of anthropological techniques be used in research designed for the historian's own purposes.

Let us take a single concrete example: W. E. F. Ward, in his *A History of the Gold Coast*[9] drew upon M. J. Field's *Social Organization of the Ga People*[10] for information on a cult, *kple*, which seemed to suggest that the cult was older in the area than the Ga invasion. But Field was not actively interested in the historical aspect of the cult and only made passing and vague references to items that could help the historian. Nevertheless, Ward, who while teaching at Achimota was actually in Ga territory, chose to base his interpretation on the (for his pur-pose) inadequate report of Field rather than using it as a point of departure for his own historiographically designed investiga-tion. The guardians and repositories of these traditions of the Ga people were his neighbours, and as accessible to him as any library.

The results of this neglected opportunity are as might be surmised: the historian has gone further than the evidence of the ethnographer warranted. J. H. Kwabena Nketia[11] by a close study of the cult and with a consideration of its history, shows that the conclusion of Ward is erroneous.

To avoid such pitfalls in the use of ethnology the historian must sometimes go beyond the previously accumulated data and by employing the field methods of the ethnographer collect data pertinent to his own purposes. The same is true of lin-guistics and other fields that are collateral to history. We will come back to the problem of how the historian should go about such ventures into other disciplines.

In the foregoing, it has been urged that unwritten sources be *added* to the written sources; this is generally accepted. It has been suggested that evidence from unwritten sources be collected; this ought to be accepted as a natural corollary. But now if we ask 'What if there are *no* written sources? Can we produce a history from unwritten sources alone? Or are unwritten sources merely ancillary to written sources and useless by themselves?'

The answer to this question is of the greatest significance for African history. It will determine how far into the past we may hope to venture. If unwritten sources are only aids, they are important and can help to enrich history for those periods for which we have written documents. But if the evidence from unwritten sources is not of the same quality as the evidence from written sources, and the former can only embellish the latter, then when the latter is missing, the former is useless; it is decoration without any structure to decorate.

If we have to accept this subordinate position for unwritten sources, then history for the Western Sudan begins with Arabic accounts, and the earlier days of Ghana must remain forever prehistoric, despite whatever accumulation the future may see of artifacts from excavations and traditions of surviving peoples. History for most other parts of Africa will necessarily begin even later, five centuries ago on the coast and in some parts of the interior less than one century.

If unwritten sources, on the other hand, yield evidence of the same quality as written sources, then our exploration of the past on this continent has no given time limitations but depends wholly upon the preservation or non-preservation of evidence.

In the second decade of this century, historians took sides on this question. Collingwood (1946) summarizes the dispute.

According to my own recollection the controversy was alive, though giving one an impression of obsolescence, in academic circles thirty years ago; all statements of the issue, so far as I can recall them, were extremely confused, . . . My impression is that the controversy fizzled out in the feeblest of compromises, the partisans of scissors-and-paste history accepting the principle that 'unwritten sources' could give valid results, but insisting that this could only happen on a very small scale and when they were used as an auxiliary arm to 'written sources'; and only about low matters like industry and commerce, into which an historian with the instincts of a gentleman would not inquire.[12]

This 'feeblest of compromises', admitting the validity of unwritten sources but hedging them with so many limitations that one need hardly consider them important, has demonstrated a

remarkable stability, despite its feebleness, for it has not yet
been swept aside. We have noted the short shrift given to unwritten sources by Gottschalk, and he is not atypical of his
generation. It is easier to find consideration in print being given
to the subject by going back to the period of the 'controversy'.
In 1911 John Martin Vincent wrote in the Preface of his
Historical Research that his 'book is offered as an outline, rather
than an encyclopaedic treatment of historical investigation',
yet in his 'outline' he managed to give a chapter of thirteen
pages of 'Evaluation of Oral Tradition' and he has another
chapter of seventeen pages on 'Relics'. Vincent gives a sympathetic attention to these unwritten sources and accords them
more space in his book than most subsequent writers addressing
the same audience, young would-be historians in college classes,
have done. But Vincent's conclusion is negative:

. . . when the materials are appraised it becomes apparent that the
relics alone are insufficient, and history would be impossible without
conscious attempts to connect its parts. The order of procedure,
therefore, is to find what has been written upon the period or topic
and then determine what light can be drawn from the collateral
material.[13]

This conclusion, whether a feeble compromise or not, that
unwritten sources are merely 'auxiliary' or 'collateral' is still
tenaciously held and I have frequently encountered it in con-
versations with historians. Collingwood, for one, and I do not
mean to imply that he is alone, manages to break out of this
limitation. He gives a parable about a Detective-Inspector
which is too long to quote here, the essence of which is that the
Detective-Inspector does not depend on what witnesses and
suspects tell him, i.e. statements about the event, equivalent to
written sources, but he can reconstruct the event from evidence
that is not *told* to him. He concludes:

I do not mean that the scientific historian can work better when no
statements are made to him about the subjects on which he is
working; . . . what I mean is that he is not dependent on such
statements being made.[14]

That is the point of view adopted here. All sources are pertinent and each that is extant should be exploited. But when
written documents are missing, it is only something to be

lamented, as the lack of any source material would be; it is not a wholly insurmountable obstacle.

In terms of our goal, to reconstruct the past, it is a great advantage to be freed of the limitations to written sources, but like any bursting of limitations, the new freedom has its own problems. How are all these various kinds of evidence to be handled with the degree of carefulness that the historian has given to written documents?

It is obvious today that it is impossible to master all knowledge. No one, historian or otherwise, can be a specialist in everything. It is necessary to choose the kind of history the individual historian wants to devote himself to. And, of course, not everyone must go in for each innovation that comes along. Social history did not put the political historian out of business, and the kind of history I am proposing will not abolish all familiar landmarks on the historical scene. A division of labour is necessary to get the broadest perspectives of history. But it will be incumbent on the historian of whatever predilection to understand the fundamentals of the new approaches, and some will have to develop the necessary breadth to attempt eventually to synthesize the results of the various approaches.

Before we consider the particular means of expansion of the scope of history, it should be noted that it is already true that one person could not hope to handle all kinds of historical evidence in current use. Note what the author of *La Société féodale* says:

As an old medievalist, I know nothing that is better reading than a cartulary. That is because I know just about what to ask it. A collection of Roman inscriptions, on the other hand, would tell me little. I know more or less how to read them, but not how to cross-question them.[15]

The choice of what materials an historian will use will be sometimes a matter of personal inclination. One may choose to examine linguistic data as another chooses to investigate economic data. But it also will be true that an historian on a geographical or ethnic basis is pushed into considering data from fields he would prefer to avoid because he has had no previous experience in those fields.

It is an axiom of research that the nature of a problem

determines the methodology. Whatever is relevant must be related to the selected historical problem, the solution of which we are seeking, and this must be done in a way that is consistent with the nature of the data. Some problems can be solved within a single discipline, but there are many that cannot. This has given rise in recent years to what has been termed inter-disciplinary research. A great deal has been written, pro and con, concerning the merits of this kind of study. Let me make it clear that I hold no special brief for inter-disciplinary research as such. My only interest is in solving problems which I consider worth the effort of their resolution.

I do not advocate bringing in a discipline just for the sake of its being represented, and certainly not so that the results will be more impressive to the general public. The only criterion which should determine whether a particular discipline will be included in an attack upon a specific problem is its ability to yield significant data on that problem. The fact that a certain discipline has been useful in solving another problem is irrelevant. The strategy of each problem must be worked out on its own terms.

An historian who starts out to investigate the history of a given locality may well find a problem which leads him off into fields of scholarship he is loath to follow—if only to begrudge the time necessary to acquire a minimum of competence. If he can find a person who is competent in the required field and willing to collaborate, he can proceed; but this has not always been easy to arrange. If he can find no such person willing to give up time from other work for the pursuance of this collaboration, the historian, if he is really interested in the solution of the problem, will begin to train himself in the necessary skills, because without them he can only continue to founder.

The organization of research on a broad scope presents special problems, and I will leave the discussion of these to the last chapter, but it will be helpful to mention here that there are at least three ways that progress can be attained. I list these in order of decreasing diffuseness: first, conferences can be convened at which individuals from different disciplines pool their information and discuss areas where their research converges; second, individuals from two or more disciplines may embark upon a project of co-operative or complementary research; and third, an individual in one discipline may set out to acquire competence in additional disciplines.

Some conservatives may object: why do you wish to burden historians with all these new difficulties? Since the data being recommended to historians already pertains to other disciplines, why shouldn't it stay there?

I have not suggested that we amputate a part of another discipline and transfer it to history. Economics was none the poorer or more restricted after historians began working on economic history. Linguists and botanists and others will continue to work on the same kinds of problems, by and large, as they did in the past, and no doubt develop some new ones. Historical work incorporating linguistic or botanical data will be in addition to, not instead of, the kinds of work being done at present.

Now, we might note that economists did not write very much economic history; the historical interest had to come from the historians. If you want new varieties of history to be developed, historians will have to take a hand in it.

Some of these fields do have a tradition of historical studies. Archaeology is wholly historical; linguistics, ethnology and some others have diachronic dimensions that have been recognized as legitimate aspects of the subject. In some of the other instances this is largely undeveloped. In any event, despite whatever historical writing is done by anthropologists, linguists or others, there is no consistent, organized medium to ensure the stimulation and circulation of such work. There are anthropologists who feel that the 'science of man' is broad enough to include every facet of human interest, and while I do not object in principle, I suggest that when you have too many irons in the fire, some of them do not get very hot.

The other pertinent fields have non-historical interests which make a continuous attention to history difficult to maintain, or if wholly historical, as is archaeology, it is only a part of the historical whole. The logical arrangement is for History as the venerable prototype of all historical studies (recognized in such designations as historical linguistics, and so on) to be the organizing centre and focus of studies in new branches of studies as it has been in the development of social and economic history.

There should be in fact no occasion for petty jurisdictional disputes between disciplines as to proprietary right. I have no more sympathy for any imperialisms of the academic world than for those of the political and military world. Intellectual work is a thing of the spirit of man; the law of matter that two things cannot occupy the same space simply does not apply. Like the angels of medieval dispute, any number of disciplines can dance on the head of a single pin.

There are many examples of two fields of inquiry that were once separate that now overlap each other but maintain their own distinctive character. As an example, we can cite theology and sociology. The former borrowed from the latter to create a sub-branch of theology called Social Ethics, while at the same time the latter was scrutinizing the former to create a new sub-branch of sociology known as the Sociology of Religion. Each may use the same data but there is a distinctly different trend of interest: Social Ethics remains theology and Sociology of Religion remains sociology.

When a field of study results from the encounter of two disciplines, it is thus important to note the direction of movement which gave rise to the hybrid. Farmers could tell us that a male ass crossed with a mare produces a mule, but that a stallion crossed with a female ass produces a hinny. Historians need not worry, if they take the initiative, that new fields of study sired out of other disciplines will have more of the other disciplines' characteristics than their own.

The kinds of data from which this new history will be extracted is different from that which the historian is now accustomed to use. It is even more unusual than that which the economic historian took for his province. The economic historian still uses documents in the narrow sense of the word, even though they may be for him tables of statistics, annual reports of commercial firms, ledger books and so on. Neither the historian (in modern times) nor the economist has made much use of the technique of going out and seeking certain types of people and interviewing them, although beginnings are being made. An example of this is Columbia University Oral History Project which is collating the voice-recordings of the opinions of today's leaders in various fields of endeavour.

Interviewing is the first step in collecting oral traditions and linguistic data which when analysed can yield historical inferences. Interviewing is not a haphazard undertaking; it has been refined to a sensitive tool of research in a number of social sciences. There are different kinds of interviewing procedures to be used, depending upon the kind of information sought. The historian who goes out to collect a series of interviews need not repeat the mistakes of early practitioners of the social sciences but can benefit from their efforts and the improved tools of investigation.

If some of the techniques are different, there is the compensation that the historical evidence is that which modern history has come to rely on more and more. All historical evidence can be divided into two categories: the first is that which is often referred to as the 'narrative sources', i.e. those which were written by authors who consciously intended to inform (or misinform) their readers. They are subject to bias and emotional pressures. The second category of evidence is that which was never intended to be examined by the historian. These may also contain some distortion. 'But this kind of distortion, if it exists, at least has not been especially designed to deceive posterity.'[16] The only kind of evidence we will be concerned with hereafter in this book that might fall into the first category is that of oral traditions.

Marc Bloch, who is one of the more cogent of modern theorists of historiography, has written,

There can be no doubt that, in the course of its development, historical research has generally been led to place more and more confidence in the second category of evidence, in the witnesses in spite of themselves. We have only to compare the Roman history of Rollins or even that of Niebuhr with any of these short summaries we read today. The former drew the heart of their matter from Livy, Suetonius, or Florus. The latter are constructed in large measure out of inscriptions, papyri, and coins. Only in this way could whole sections of the past have been reconstructed. This is true of all prehistory, as well as almost all economic history and almost all history of social structures.[17]

It was in learning to use these 'witnesses in spite of themselves' and putting together in a kind of puzzle small scraps of information from various sources that history became, as Michelet put it, less the unmoving pupil of the chronicles of the ancients and more the ever-daring explorer of all ages.

Linguistics offers what is perhaps the most unconscious evidence of any that is pertinent to history; and no one would seriously suggest that the inhabitants of an old site planned their ruins in such a way as to influence an archaeologist's interpretations. It is important before we look at the various kinds of evidence (that form the subject of succeeding chapters) that we understand that these are historical evidences of the best kind, even though until now largely neglected by historians, and they are good evidence because they have not been arranged for us by human actors with motives to sway our judgement. This is not to say that there are no weaknesses in these kinds of evidence, that they do not often lack the definiteness of written documents, and so on. We will have to consider the problems of evaluating and interpreting each of the varieties of evidence in subsequent chapters.

We are not, then, going to be talking about things which are only related to history by a great stretch of the imagination, things that have been dragged in, like King Charles' head, out of all context. We will be talking about things which are the real stuff of history, even if not always recognized as such. And the time is not far off, I venture to predict, when many historians will think it just as natural to work with glottochronologies, stool and drum histories, and studies of pot-sherds as other historians have learned to work with national budgets and custom office receipts. The lead, in fact, has already been taken by some historians of ancient and medieval times, and probing efforts have begun in the search for Africa's history.

It is essential to the reconstruction of Africa's past that the methodology of collecting and cross-examining unwritten documents be established on as firm a basis as has that for using written documents. We need not pause to consider those who have essayed to write African history from any and all sources with little more to guide them than their own enthusiasm. African history until recently received little recognition in the universities, and being relegated to the amorphous limbo of extra-curricular pastimes or the hobby of the non-academic individual of intellectual inclination, there has been a disproportionate amount of writing by amateurs. I do not repudiate all amateurs. To some we owe a great deal of enlightenment; to others we can only attribute unfortunate confusion.

African history must be organized into a discipline and incorporated into the academic structure to provide a yardstick for the work of those part-time enthusiasts who give their main working hours to other professions. The establishment of African history on a firm academic basis will not discourage the amateur, in the original sense of the word, but will be of assistance to him as well as to the professional historian; and, I believe, there will always be a place for the amateur who comes to his historical interest often late in life but by innate talent and application makes up his deficiencies in training.

The evidence from each type of source requires handling appropriate to itself. That is to say, that the nature of one kind of evidence is different from that of another. Myths, excavated tools, starred forms of a proto-language are all quite distinct types of data. Will not the nature of the data, then, affect work which the historian can produce from such evidence? How closely will a diachronic narrative derived from unwritten sources resemble what we know as history?

One of the characteristics of such history is the paucity of individual names and figures that appear. Only from oral traditions can we get named individuals. From excavations we may learn of individuals who by the splendour of their burials were obviously great and powerful persons and by giving them epithets of some sort we may grace our narratives with a measure of the individual personality. But on the whole, the focus of history produced from unwritten sources is on the society rather than on individuals. It is, in a certain sense, one step higher in abstraction. To give an example, it is more like the history of Minoan Crete than it is like that of Classical Greece. It seems to me a reasonable contention that there is a place for this kind of study in the field of history.

It can be misleading, however, to say that this society-focused history is a higher abstraction than a persons-focused history, for that might imply that we had derived the higher level of abstraction from the lower, and could therefore make deductions from the higher back to the lower. This is not true in this case, of course, as data on individuals has been unobtainable (except from burials and oral traditions); and in any case, abstracting from data on individuals would give us an abstraction of individuality. Society is more than a collection of individuals; it is also the organization of interaction between them, both the formal and informal patterns. The difference between society and individuals is as distinct as that between physiology and body chemistry. We can understand the functioning of a particular organ without knowing the chemical processes that are involved, and so we can understand social organization without knowing all the significant things about personality norms and deviation from these norms, to say nothing of the complexity of a single individual within the society. Thus we are dealing with a more inclusive level of organization, but our knowledge was not derived from the subordinate level and we cannot by ratiocination alone make the transition from the one level to the other.

Although some philosophers might be quite content that history derived from unwritten sources is more abstract than most other examples of history, as historians we cannot but lament that the focus on individuals is often beyond our reach. If we could have our wish, we would like to have both; we do not want to choose or to make invidious comparisons between them: each has its own worth, and full understanding only comes with an appreciation of both. When we have only the society-focused history, it is because under these circumstances it is all that is available to us, and that in itself is an enormous achievement. We would like to hope, without being able to see the possible means of its fulfilment, that some day we will learn to recover the personal level of history as we have learned to uncover the societal.

Some followers of certain deterministic schools might even take the high and mighty stand that the individual is unimportant and that history without him is more scientific. If I could believe this, I would be a great deal more satisfied with the kind of history I am going to expostulate, but that would not be an achievement as much as it would be soporific.

Carlyle[18] stands at one end and Plekhanov[19] at the other of extremes in interpretation of the role of the individual in the history. To the former he is everything; to the latter, nothing. If we could agree on this with the latter, the individual would cease to concern us; we would have no problem on this score and could get on with other things. If we had to agree with the former, we would be forced to renounce as useless everything that follows in the later parts of this book. Few historians today stand at either of these extremes. Most of us would be cautious in employing any factor in an historical interpretation and definitely avoid reliance on a single factor for explanation although we might feel that one factor in certain instances was more important than the others. We have learned to be sceptical of extremes and of determinisms. The determinists, be they geographical, economic, or cultural, have made some good points, but they have gone too far in their reliance on a single factor. The very fact that there are several distinct schools based on quite different determinisms indicates that each of these factors could not be as all-important as is claimed and probably that none of them is.

The geographical condition can provide or withhold certain prerequisites for various types of pursuits in a given community, but it does not, by itself, indicate the development of any of the community's innate potentialities, and we know that there are peoples with quite different ways of life who live in similar environments. This earliest school of determinism is now virtually defunct, but we have learned from the arguments they engendered to look for geographical prerequisites without attributing to them motivational force.

The economic structure is only one of the institutional structures within a society. Economic determinists often seem to equate economic structure with the total system of societal structures. It can be shown that some of the other institutional forms will change in response to economic changes, e.g. family structure (both in drawing the boundaries of membership, i.e. a choice between an extended or a nuclear family, and in the roles of the members) has been altered in a number of cases in different societies as a function of occupational change. Certainly, the economic institutions are a vital and dynamic part of a society, perhaps even the most important single aspect of the society in forming its character, but it is not the totality, and we cannot fully comprehend a society by its economics alone. Max Weber[20] believed that religion influenced economic structure, and he still has many followers. In this, if not in everything, I am more inclined to lean towards Emile Durkheim,[21] and see the religious structure, in much the same fashion as the family, responding to adjust itself to structural changes in the economy. However, the relationship of the political structure to the economy is not as simple as the Marxists, who are only one of the schools of economic determinism, see it: although it is demonstrable that economic interests in the society influence the government, and sometimes even capture it; it is equally true that government can influence the economy even to the extent of dictating to, or expropriating, industry and other segments of the economy. In either of the extreme cases a distinction is meaningless. The old term of political-economy was a good one inasmuch as it indicated a duality and an equity in a loose integration. The economic determinists who are still writing tend to be, for the most part, ideologists of a political philosophy rather than primarily historians, and thus are of relatively little influence in the field.

The latest of the determinisms, 'culturology', has had little influence and is not likely to have. Historians long ago recognized, if they did not greatly develop, the concept of national character, which is, of course, the effect of culture on personality. A closer exchange between the more cogent of the personality-in-culture school (C. Arensberg's paper to the New York Academy of Science) with the national character historians would seem to be more promising than the cultivation of another determinism. Actually some of the ideas of culturology have already been examined and discarded under another guise. *Zeitgeist,* which can be an acceptable term if confined to the meaning of the ethos, or cultural values of a given place and time, was used too ambitiously formerly by some scholars, particularly in Germany, who attempted to explain all actions by a rather mechanical application of this concept. Culturology, a pedantic term at best, is not likely to have greater effect on history than the proponents of *Zeitgeist.* Culturologists are also evolutionists and so may contribute to the history of institutions. In as much as some of them make use of the concept of social energy they seem to approach economic history.

The truth is that an individual lives within a set of geographical circumstances, a particular economy, and a definite culture, and all of these things have some effect upon him, but no one of them, nor all of them together, can fully explain an individual, nor the range of individuals' tastes and types. Perhaps some day we will be able to give a full explanation, but we cannot really claim to do so today. Yet if we can doubt that the external forces completely dominate the individual, we can be sure that the individual does not dominate the external forces. No one today could intelligently and seriously follow the ebullient, idealistic optimism of Carlyle in this regard. Institutions are not typically the lengthened shadow of one man, nor is history the shadow of heroes, but without the action of individuals, and heroic individuals, historical processes would not take place.

Whereas Plekhanov said that if it had not been Napoleon it would have been another general, Napoleon had a different view. 'La chance est aussi une qualité,' he said. Luck does not befall everyone: why did Bonaparte win battles? Why was he called by the Directory instead of 'some other general'?

In amplification of this view, we might say that something of historical importance happens to individuals who put themselves in a position where it can happen; that the call to leadership comes from outside the individual but only to the individual who has prepared himself for that leadership, of whatever type it may be. This is the real explanation of the 'charismatic' leader whether it be Sitting Bull, Cromwell, the leader of the Taipings, or modern leaders. *Charisma* is not an aspect of a stable social organization, but is 'a pattern taken by movements of change as such'.[22]

Louis Pasteur expressed the same idea in a slightly different way. He was asked if all scientific discoveries were not the result of accidents. Perhaps so, he admitted, but you must examine the lives of the people to whom these accidents happen. When the same thing is discovered independently and more or less simultaneously by two or more individuals, we can see the part played respectively by the actor and the *milieu* more distinctly than where we deal with a unique achievement. The telephone, the steamship, the automobile, the movie camera could each be independently invented not merely because of a *Zeitgeist*, or focus of attention on the problem, nor simply because a complex invention utilizes a number of accomplishments of the past ready at hand to be used. Yet we would not like to make the teleological suggestion that the need of society at the moment called the thing into being; the individuals who brought the instruments to a degree of perfection to permit efficient operation had to be immersed in the problem to an extent not typical of their neighbours. Again we note that Darwin and Wallace studied nature while their contemporaries discussed evolution in the drawing-rooms.

The geographical, economic, and cultural compulsions seem to have differentially affected the different individuals. Genius, by itself, is an insufficient explanation because it does not seem plausible that two geniuses would appear at the same moment and turn their attention to the same item rather than to any of the other innumerable possibilities for the outlet of their talents. The *milieu* channels the activity of the genius to a certain extent, but if there were not extra-ordinary individuals, would the *milieu* be able to accomplish the same ends?

It seems to me that there can be no doubt that both the individual and all the things that define the *milieu* are important to history, and we must therefore strive to obtain a history of societies and their outstanding individuals. That is why oral traditions are so important among the unwritten sources when we are lacking any written evidence. And we admit furthermore that a history derived from unwritten sources tends to be less complete than that for which we have literary sources. We can in fact make divisions of history on the basis of the nature and amplitude of our sources of evidence. Literate periods are the fullest in detail and the most susceptible to verification, partly because we can here use all the unwritten sources as well; non-literate periods where we have certain unwritten types of evidence can approach, at times, but never equal the literate periods in detail and verification; and remote periods, where contact with living people is no longer possible and the sources of evidence are few and limited, such as the Old Stone Ages, fall well short even of this middle range. The task we are concerned with here is how to rediscover as much as possible of this middle range.

We must admit, then, that history without individuals, or with limited information on individuals, is incomplete. But history is always incomplete. The objection might be raised, if one were to take an extreme position, that without individuals this is not history at all. Collingwood says, 'All history is the history of thought.'[23] Does this mean that a narrative of the past without individuals, i.e. the thinkers, is not history? Not at all; the evidence of the thought can be perceived even when the thinker can not. Taylor[24] demonstrates that behind an artifact is an idea; the material object is evidence of thought. Admittedly this does not give us the full range of thought, but it gives us the thought pertinent to the societal level which is all that we are claiming to reconstruct.

Let us look at the term 'recoverable history'. What is recoverable? That depends on our techniques. As our techniques improve, the limits of recoverable history are extended. Much of what will be discussed in later chapters was not long ago beyond the hope of recovery. We should maintain a flexibility, and a hopefulness, in our attitude towards the unknown, and we should aggressively pursue even the smallest lead and continuously strive to improve existing techniques and to find and develop new ones.

The benefits will be not merely the elucidation of the history of Africa but an enrichment of history itself. When these branches of history are developed, we will certainly find that they will be employed for countries so rich in documents they haven't yet felt the need to look in these directions. That the history of Europe can be supplemented by unwritten sources is already indicated by a few straws in the wind. For example, Menendez-Pidal made a contribution to the *political* history (which is the most amply cultivated part of history) of Spain by an analysis of the vocabulary of the Spanish language.[25]

For Africa the development of unwritten sources of history is an absolute necessity, and some day when the methodology of this kind of history has been perfected, we may consider this one of Africa's contributions to the world. It appears to me that it is one of the great opportunities of African universities to cultivate this promising field.

In summary, then, our thesis is that historical evidence is any analysable survival from the past, and that there are not only kinds of data but methods of research to be derived from the various subdivisions of anthropology. These are not only pertinent but indispensable to the reconstruction of history in areas and periods where reliance must be put on unwritten sources of evidence. Results of such work are truly a part of history, which is an ever-expanding search for knowledge of man's past.

Thus our knowledge of the earlier stages of human culture has been built up with the aid of scientists in several disciplines—the geologist, palaeontologist, zoologist, soil chemist, and botanist, for example. Just as the help of the human anatomist is essential for the interpretation of the nature of a particular fossil skull, so is the help of these other scientists, and it is only by enlisting their aid in interpreting the evidence collected by the prehistorian that we shall be able to arrive in the end at a clearer picture of human evolution.

J. Desmond Clark

CHAPTER TWO

ARMED WITH A SPADE . . .

THE order in which we take the various fields to be discussed is arbitrary. I have decided to begin with archaeology for three reasons. First, no one doubts that it is pertinent to history. Secondly, it has a tested scientific methodology, matched for vigour only by linguistics. And finally, archaeology does not hesitate to incorporate skills and judgements from a dozen other fields. In this last respect, it can serve as a model for the kind of history I advocated in the preceding chapter.

Archaeology uses geology; due to the work of Lyell and Agassiz its importance for chronology is realized. The surveyor and architect contribute their skills to recording the dimensions of the site and its structures. The metallurgist, zoologist and paleontologist analyse metallic artifacts and bones that are exhumed. The draughtsman, photographer and clerks record the finds. Laboratory technicians test and preserve them. All these functions have to be fulfilled as well as that of the gang of shovel handlers. The analyses of stone and ceramic artifacts are almost invariably the inalienable province of the archaeologist but for any other tasks he may have to rely upon another member of the team or even an outside expert. In practice, any number of combinations of these functions is possible, depending on the versatility of the particular archaeologist and the amplitude of his finances.

One of the disadvantages of archaeology is that it is expensive, and this is inescapable since excavation is a team operation. The historian is apt to think it fantastically costly, but an archaeologist is more likely to put it into a better perspective. 'Archaeology is a relatively expensive form of research, though far cheaper than astronomy or nuclear physics.'[1]

Money may be raised in a single large grant, from a government, foundation or an individual philanthropist, or it may be raised, piecemeal, in small amounts from various sources, or even by subscriptions by interested persons or groups, clubs and societies. In the latter case, historians could be of assistance to archaeologists in popularizing the appeal of the fund-raising.

The origin of the money tends to put some pressure on the archaeologist. The individual benefactor may be eccentric and have exotic theories he hopes to vindicate. A donating government may be interested in influencing the interpretation for what it considers to be national glory. A foundation may have bureaucratic regulations about how the money can be spent. If there are 'strings attached' to money, these ought to be recognized before acceptance.

Archaeological studies may be divided into categories by the typical kind of artifact that characterizes them. The three larger categories reflect stages of technological development: stone, ceramic, and metal. These categories are in the order of most ancient to the more recent, and also of increasing quantity and complexity of remains.

The Paleolithic is known to us only through the medium of stone and bone and the range of implements, though wide, is limited. Rock painting, where extant, is the only supplement to stone technology. Almost everything, therefore, beyond technology, that is asserted about the life of Stone Age men is inference and conjecture. It is primarily ethnology which provides a basis for interpreting palaeolithic finds.

The Neolithic is a more promising field for the historian's effort, though less so than the metal-using, state-forming period. The Neolithic is characterized by larger populations and usually larger settlements. The increased population is due to the mastery of food-producing techniques—plant cultivation and/ or the domestication of animals. In fact, it is food production rather than the polishing of stone (which originally gave the name to this period) that is today considered important. Indeed it is the leisure afforded by the improved food supply, rather than greater skill, which permitted stone polishing which was largely aesthetic rather than practical in its purpose.

Most Neolithic sites have pot-sherds as well as polished stone. Ceramic styles show greater variability than stone techniques and tool styles and so are a better indicator of local differentiation. Pots sometimes show relationships to existing or historic peoples and so permit a contact between literary history and archaeology.

Ceramics also makes possible a preservable plastic art. Terracotta figurines may illustrate perishable items like clothing, and group figures may represent social situations such as work scenes, homage to a chief, or marriage ceremonies. Sometimes this is extensively developed by a group. One Peruvian people are said to have written their own ethnology in clay.

Whereas the Neolithic is a distinct break with the preceding Paleolithic, the metal ages are a continuation and development of the possibilities of the Neolithic; but at a point which cannot be precisely marked by the presence or absence of metal, a revolution in social organization sometimes occurs. This is what V. G. Childe called the urban revolution. Once this has taken place, the fundamental basis of the type of society with which the historian is familiar is present, and it therefore becomes easier for him to perceive such a society in the series of societies that are known to history.

The Greeks called the city-state πολις and we see how all-pervasive this has been by the variety of derived words. *Politics* and *policy* are still relatively close to the original concept, as is *police*, though with a different emphasis. *Politeness* distinguishes the city-bred person from the peasant. *Urbane* was derived from Latin by a similar reasoning. But the Latin equivalent was really *civitas* rather than *urbs*, which gives us *civil* and even *civilization* itself.

The State, only relatively recently distinguished from the city, which is still its focus, is, from the city-state to the nation-state, one of the primary concerns of history. The problem of states and state-formation have not been given enough attention in Africa, but D. Westermann has identified sixty-four instances south of the Sahara of what he called 'state building societies'.[2]

Many of these African states are very inadequately known; but in proportion to the richness of a site, excavation could do for them what it has done, for example, for the Etruscans, about whom we know no more from classical historical sources than we usually know from oral tradition about an extinct African state. Pallottino,[3] one of the foremost Etruscologists today, refers to his study as paleoethnology. If it has been profitable in the Mediterranean to combine ethnology (in an amount larger than usual) with archaeology, it will probably be obvious that this should be so south of the Sahara. And here we have a relative richness, for although the continent is too vast to be thoroughly covered by ethnographic studies, those that exist are on the average of an excellent quality.

We cannot avoid mentioning any longer that there are two somewhat different breeds of archaeologists. One might be called the art-oriented archaeologist and the other the anthropology-oriented archaeologist. The former can hardly be lured away from the Eastern and Central Mediterranean, Egypt and the Middle East, but some have ventured to southern or eastern Asia. Sites without the likelihood of exquisite statuary and massive architecture are not worthy of their notice. The second type is exemplified by those who have excavated American Indian settlement sites and sometimes found not a single artifact surviving from the meagre Amerindian material culture, but were not discouraged but were happy if they were able to determine the settlement pattern. The postholes of the dwellings revealed this even though the wood had rotted away; the replaced soil was of a different colour from the surrounding matrix. Sutton Hoo in England and some Danish sites required as much attention to small detail and careful analysis.

The point does not need to be laboured that in attracting archaeologists to work in Africa preference should be given to the anthropology-oriented rather than to the art-oriented. This is a matter of attitude rather than of the sites one has worked on. Many an archaeologist who has never worked on any but an art-rich site may be none the less anthropology-oriented. The criterion is the manner in which they regard certain tedious details which can never yield artistic objects but which might provide a clue to chronology or to some aspect of the daily life of common people. For example, Sir Mortimer Wheeler took to task some eminent excavators of the 'Holy Lands' who claimed that stratigraphy could not be determined in a site where earth buildings (pisé, adobe, or 'swish') had crumbled. He charged them with insufficient interest in the problem. Although he didn't so designate this fault, it is what I have called art-orientation. Stratigraphy can generally be determined in such a site but it requires a close and continuous attention.

Building with earth is so common in Africa that this is an important consideration, but no hard and fast rules can be set down. There are sometimes situations where stratigraphy *is* impossible. At Ifé, Frank Willett found that although different pottery styles undoubtedly represented different periods, these were found all indifferently mixed together from the highest to the lowest levels of the excavation. The explanation is that the site has been so continuously built over for such a long time that collapsed walls and former lanes between houses (and all the broken pot-sherds lying about) have been incorporated in new walls, not once but several times.

In general, we may expect that sites in Africa will be what are sometimes called 'mute' sites, that is, that they will not yield inscriptions or other written materials; but this will not be invariably true, and archaeologists and historians ought to be on the lookout for writings of various kinds. Only two indigenous scripts, Meroitic and Old Libyan (and its offshoot Tifinath), are likely to be found, and neither had a wide dispersal; but Arabic script, sometimes as a vehicle for African languages, is a much more widespread possibility. De Menziéres is said to have found a *tarikh* in the walls of Kumbi Salah but this seems to have disappeared, perhaps during World War I. Jack Goody more recently directed attention to the existence of chronicles in Arabic script still in use in northern Ghana. Epigraphy is thus not excluded from the continent. Phillip Curtin has suggested that we must revise our attitude towards the Sudan; it is not proper to regard it as a non-literate region. We regard medieval Europe differently and yet all but a handful of the Europeans of that time were illiterate. The medieval Sudan, like medieval Europe, had its handful of 'clerks' who wrote and copied manuscripts. The disorganization of the societies of the western Sudan subsequent to 1591 has resulted in the disappearance of many of these books, but enough have survived to provide, when assembled and analysed, a purview of Sudanic history which will be, we hope, comparable in many ways to that we have obtained by much diligent research of medieval European history.

Numismatics is likewise sometimes thought to have little scope in African archaeology. That it will be limited is true, but it may be a surprise to many to realize how widely coins have been found in Africa. Thousands of coins, including several coin-hoards, have come to light along the East African coast. Maghrabine coins have been found at Gao, on the Niger, where Kufic inscriptions were also found. All along the fringe of the Islamic world coins might be found, and although the chances are usually slim, it is an important possibility because coins are good time-markers and indicators of trade connexions.

Until just a few years ago, there were only about half a dozen sites outside of Egypt and North Africa that had been excavated on this vast continent and some of these were only exploratory trenches. Fortunately there has lately been a steady increase in the number of archaeologists attached to universities, research institutes, and governments in various parts of Africa, and gradually the quantity of data is increasing. What can the historian do with the archaeologists' material?

Often the historian has been content to take the conclusions of the archaeologist and tack them on as a kind of preface to his history. For some purposes this may be sufficient, but often it is not. He can certainly go beyond this, but to do so he must understand how the archaeologist works.

To the archaeologist, 'culture is an assemblage of artifacts'. He must make a classification of the types of artifacts, plot their frequencies, distribution and sequence. When he has the classification of types (and their frequencies) he can describe the culture. When he has compared his site with others (wherever comparison seems fruitful) he may have deduced something of the pattern of contacts. When he has the established succession of cultures for a given site he knows something of the pattern of change.

At all stages of the interpretation, he must build inferences. In doing this, he does not rely only upon the materials he has disinterred, but he makes use of a wide reading not only in archaeological reports, but in history and ethnology and whatever may be relevant. It is generally true, that the wider the reading, the sounder the inferences. Fortunately, archaeologists are almost always familiar with the works of historians, at least for the area in which they are working. The reverse ought to be true, but it generally is not; historians usually have only the slightest acquaintance with the reports of archaeological excavations that have been done in the area of their specialization.

When an archaeologist writes his report, it becomes a public property that any historian can pursue by visiting a library. Historians ought to study all archaeological reports on the area of their interest and compare them with comparable reports on related areas. The nature of archaeological reports, the necessity of almost interminable minute descriptions of fragments of pots and other objects, makes them tedious, and no one, not even an archaeologist, can sit down and read one through. It should generally be treated as a catalogue rather than a narrative; but the catalogue is there as a reference for the various steps in the interpretation, and the serious reader will not restrict himself to the conclusions, but will check back to the drawings and descriptions of the artifacts.

When an historian comes upon something that seems significant for his own work, he should try to follow the reasoning in the inferences that are drawn and should check for himself the general conclusions. This is in no way improper and is only what he would do in judging a fellow historian's work.

The excavator has an advantage which no other person can subsequently share. He has lived with the site and watched the excavation through its stages. He has pondered the artifacts as he held them and examined them. The reader of his report is several removes from this reality. None the less, it is true that there are some good excavators who are poor interpreters of the excavated material. These two phases are distinct. One need not have done the excavation to attempt an interpretation. All science is based on the open acceptance of review by independent minds. An excavation is not a chemical experiment that can be replicated but the report can be critically re-assessed.

If historians took this upon themselves, they would not only be surer of the conclusions of the archaeologist when they adopted them, but they might sometimes be able to offer alternate interpretations.

There is already the beginning of a rapprochement between history and archaeology in Europe and America. The medieval field system has been revealed by archaeological methods; genre wood carving under old church pews sometimes tell as much of the life of commoners as written records do. An iron foundry only three hundred years old was excavated in my home town in Massachusetts which revealed an aspect of colonial life. The rebuilding of Colonial Williamsburg in Virginia is an encouraging example of the co-operation of archaeologists and historians. Archaeology is being employed in areas where historians have quantities of written records; historians cannot afford not to make full use of the possibilities of archaeology where the written evidence is limited.

Can the historian undertake excavations if no archaeologist is available? In Britain, amateurs have worked on Roman and Saxon sites. This is one of the finest examples of the British penchant for intellectual hobbies. But the dangers of amateur archaeology must be clearly pointed out. If a site is damaged, the evidence is absolutely irreplaceable. In most countries, laws protect certain classes of antiquities from amateur bungling. Laws of this kind should be instituted in African countries wherever they are not already in effect, and their enforcement should be encouraged. Then if an amateur has prepared himself for his task and has obtained the permission of authorities responsible for antiquities in the country he can proceed.

It would be a good thing for history students on their summer vacations to work with an archaeological team. This could often be arranged quite easily and would be good experience. The use of unpaid amateurs is one way of cutting down the high costs of excavation.

A new development is underwater archaeology.[4] Some work has already been done off North Africa's Mediterranean coast, where a Phoenician harbour was studied and the cargo of a Roman ship recovered. The sea corrodes some things but preserves others. What is lost in the sea is at least safe from grave robbers and other plunderers. Rising coastlines and a shallow continental shelf in western Africa perhaps remove a large area from the scope of marine excavations, but the Canary Islands have drowned shores where perhaps evidence of early contacts might be found. The Indian Ocean coast, too, ought to be interesting to explore for the debris of ancient trade.

There are a number of good books by archaeologists which explain their subject to the layman. Archaeology, in fact, has been blessed with a number of lucid writers who have 'popularized' their field without emasculating it. Historians should give these books a prominent place on their shelves.

PRINCE:	I do not like the Tower, of any place.
	Did Julius Caesar build that place, my lord?
BUCKINGHAM:	He did, my gracious lord, begin that place;
	Which, since, succeeding ages have re-edified.
PRINCE:	Is it upon record, or else reported
	Successively from age to age, he built it?
BUCKINGHAM:	Upon record, my gracious lord.
PRINCE:	But say, my lord, it were not register'd,
	Methinks the truth should live from age to age,
	As 'twere retail'd to all posterity,
	Even to the general all-ending day.

Richard III, Act III Scene 1

CHAPTER THREE

THE HERITAGE OF THE EARS

THERE were three reasons for giving archaeology precedence: it is accepted as related to history; it has a tested methodology; and it is able to incorporate the data of auxiliary disciplines without confusion. Only one of these applies to oral traditions: they are generally thought in some way to be related to history. But after a century of increasingly meticulous work which has brought many refinements to the study of orally transmitted lore, we have yet to reach a consensus of specialists on methods of study of historical traditions, and even on whether such traditions have value to history.

The first thing we must determine is what comes under the rubric of oral traditions, and then which categories of oral tradition, if any, are significant for historical research.

Any lore of whatever nature that is passed down verbally from one generation to the succeeding generation may be considered oral tradition; it is what the Hova of Madagascar call 'The Heritage of the Ears'. A more widespread, if less picturesque, term is *folklore*, coined in 1846 by William J. Thoms, and subsequently taken over by other languages, as for example in French, where *le folklore* and the adjective *folklorique* are now as much at home as *contes populaires* or other synonyms.

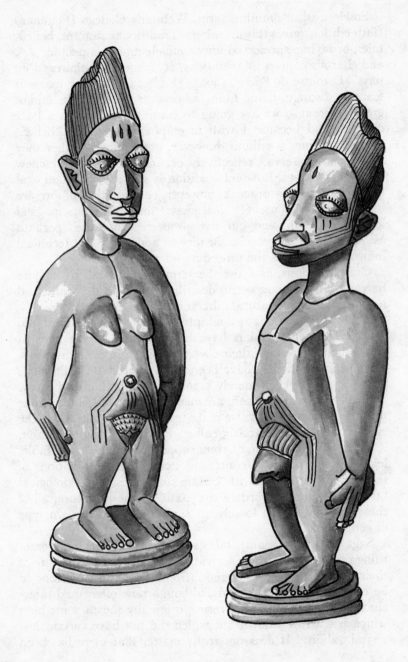

Folklore is an omnibus term. Webster's College Dictionary (fifth edition) gives this meaning: 'Traditional customs, beliefs, tales, or sayings, preserved unreflectively among a people . . .'; and Larousse gives: 'Traditions et usages populaires d'un pays' [Larousse de Poche, 1960]. This broad meaning makes it scarcely distinguishable from *folkways*, or indeed from ethnography. Because we are going to consider customs in a later chapter, and because I wish to emphasize here the 'beliefs, tales, or sayings' (without, however, prejudging whether they have been preserved reflectively or unreflectively), I eschew the word folklore. But oral tradition is still a very broad and unprecise term. In practice, however, certain kinds of lore are usually given separate treatment; for example, magical formulae of supposed curative properties and the (perhaps associated) herbal specifics for illness; and in general technical information such as the procedure for making a canoe.

Oral traditions, as I use the term, may be taken as those narratives which purport to describe or explain the world and its natural or supernatural inhabitants.

There have been many attempts to divide oral traditions into classes. Different scholars have had widely different ends in view when they made their classifications, and in many cases, perhaps in most, they have been more interested in 'literary', ethnological, or even merely taxonymic goals than in history. Some of these classifications are inevitably not well suited to our purposes, but in so far as we make use of existing collections, the system of classification of the collector will require our attention.

Terms which one may come upon are myth, saga, fable, legend, tale, märchen, conte and story, and combinations of these or other nouns with certain adjectives, e.g. etiological tale, local legend, pourquoi story, etc. In the literature, all of these terms are often loosely used, and each has its own type of confusion.

Saga (something said), tale (something told), conte (something recounted) by their derivation indicate the oral nature of their subject matter; but legend (from L. *legenda*, something to be read; from *legere*, to read), although now often used interchangeably with the other terms, originally meant something which was written down but which did not have certain historical validity. It does not really matter that there has been such an extension of the latter term, especially since written accounts have fed all the literature in the past in Europe and Asia, as you know from many documented instances. But it is important to us that neither general usage nor etymology give us sufficient clues to the meaning as employed in a particular instance, and we have to give special attention to the meaning assigned by the author. To add to the difficulty, this is not always clearly indicated; even when it is, it may not be consistently followed by the author himself.

I would divide narratives into four classes. (1) Stories concerning the supernatural, the activities of deities, spirits and semi-divine heroes, and the origin of the world, mankind, and cultural artifacts and institutions which usually are said to have been achieved through the instrumentality of these sacred beings. These stories are intimately related to the religion of the people. This type of story, I would designate as myth. (Myth is used in quite another way by some scholars, and we will look at their ideas of the ritual-myth relationship later.) (2) Etiological stories explaining the local environment and the nature of animals. These may be merged into the myths as defined above, but they may be distinct, i.e. lacking the religious quality. These are a sort of natural history. (3) Stories of what was done by the ancestors, and the people with whom they were in contact. These are the traditional tribal and family histories. (4) There may also be widely known stories about characters, not deified and not claimed as ancestors. These may be told solely for entertainment. Such characters may be the personification of a particular trait or a generalized exaggeration, like Paul Bunyan, or they may be more normal but receive wondrous assistance, like Dick Whittington. But it is not usually easy to be sure that such stories have always been purely for amusement, and therefore in practice it is a sometimes delicate decision to separate these from the other types of stories.

The dividing lines, in fact, between all of these categories are far from distinct. The *personae* proper to the first class, *myth*, may regularly intrude into the other classes. Class two, *etiological stories*, may in some societies become completely absorbed into myth if the alleged etiology always derives from the activities of sacred beings. Class three, *tribal and family traditions*, is normally invaded by the supernatural; deities help the ancestors, but it is clear that the emphasis of the narrative is upon the ancestors and that the supernatural helpers are merely auxiliaries. We can thus usually isolate these traditions without too much difficulty. Class four, *entertaining stories*, by their nature are not as likely to be involved with the sacred beings of myth. None the less, we may be dealing with desacralized myth, which after a religious revolution remained to begin a new life in new contexts. Other contaminations, such as class two with class three, which would not be serious, or class three and class four, which could be very puzzling, are also possible.

It should be clear that this classification is one which we, as outside observers, place upon the materials of oral traditions. It is a typological classification which should be applicable to the traditions of any people. Now we should always try to find out if the people whose traditions we are studying had any system of classification of their own, and if so we must determine just what it was before we attempt any analysis. A number of peoples, in fact, have names for the different types of stories that they tell, and these names are important because they tell us that in the culture of this people there is a conscious (i.e. publicly recognized) category. For the people for whom such named types of stories have been recorded, the categories will generally fit in with the typology outlined above, although they do not necessarily have all of them. However, we must still be cautious because the systematization of traditions among a particular people may undergo modification. New types may come in or old ones be dropped, and in the process the content of a discarded or neglected category of story may be remodelled in a tale that fits into a different category.

Wilhelm Grimm long ago pointed out that some tales told for amusement are broken-down myths.[1] Although we need not go all the way with him when he asserts that myth 'seems to have formed the only subject of the oldest fictions', we can none the less find numerous cases wherein a former myth has lost all but its ludic function.

How many of these categories are important for history?

The first, the myths, are religiously, rather than historically, oriented. They are of concern to students of comparative religion, of course, and perhaps also to psychologists as examples of perception and outlook; but as they deal with the supernatural, are they not obviously outside the history of man? From at least two considerations, the religious myths of a people are pertinent to their history. First, religion tends to sacerdotolize the more important institutions in a society. Authority is sanctified by godhood and priesthood (this is certainly so in Africa where 'divine-kings' are common); thus the study of the religion aids in a study of the political and social structure and we need not tell historians of the importance of political structure. Secondly, sometimes the deities may be ancestors or heroes who have been 'elevated' into the supernatural and their exploits may indicate human actions of historical significance. Another way in which human action may be attributed to deities is through the identity of priest and deity which results in stories of what priests did being attributed to the god they represent. The conflict of gods may thus be a conflict of human groups who use these symbols. Comparative study of the myths of cognate peoples may permit us, in some cases, to separate the human from the divine and the historical from the theological.

The second category, etiological stories, is unscientific natural history but not human history and can be generally ignored, but possible relationship to myth should be considered.

The third category, tribal and family traditional histories, are the most likely pay-dirt. They have the greatest resemblance to history. They assert beliefs about descent, succession to office of chiefs or kings, migrations, battles and so on. Yet there are many people who deny any reliability to 'oral history'. And we shall have to examine their objections.

The fourth category, tales and anecdotes for amusement, all will agree is non-historical, if not demoted myth or tribal history.

A very large part of the study of folklore has centred on tales for entertainment: Hansel and Gretel, Cinderella, The Star Husband and the Tar-baby. Many of the systems of classification of folktales make many distinctions within this category, see for example, *Verzichnis der Märchentypen*.[2] But these have a limited usefulness for us. The tales have a history and this in itself is interesting and, if it can be recovered, is a part of the intellectual and cultural history of the people.[3]

Elements within tales have been analysed and a *Motif-Index*

of Folk Literature in six volumes has been prepared by Stith
Thompson.[4] Although the index is not complete, in as much as
so much of the world's oral traditions are still unrecorded, and
Africa is but poorly represented in the index, it can nevertheless be useful as a preliminary check whether the motif is
unique or has a certain distribution over various regions and
among various peoples. In so far as these motifs are found in
Märchen they are useful, as stated above, for the intellectual
history; but they may also intrude into tribal or family traditions and the reason or circumstances given for an action in a
narrative may be a cultural stereotype of a kind that may be
found in their Märchen. This does not invalidate the authen-
ticity of the action itself, but we must discount the alleged
motivation for the action. For example, *The Iliad* attributed the
Trojan War to the abduction of Helen, but modern scholars
would tend to accept the war as a fact but reject the alleged
cause. The Greeks had a tendency to attribute war to this
particular motivation and Herodotus lists several cases in the
opening passages of his History. Such an index, and we will
have to compile an adequate one for Africa, will help us to
separate such stylized elements from the 'true' action of the
narrative.

In dealing with the oral traditions of a people, we should
view them as a whole and not assume that we can make facile
decisions as to what can be discarded. Any part of the 'heritage
of the ears' may be indispensable; we cannot know in advance
what will be necessary to the solution of a problem. In addition
to the narratives themselves, a proverb or a riddle may provide
the key to the interpretation of a myth. An anecdote may
instruct us about states of mind which may be central to a
family tradition. And not only do we want to attempt to comprehend the traditions of a people in their entirety, but we need
also to see them in relation to those of their neighbours and even
of the world. This is an ideal, and as such not completely
realizable. But traditions diffuse; they may be borrowed by
peoples who originally had nothing to do with them, and only
by analyses of elements and of distributions of whole tales and
of constituent elements will we be able to assess the place of a
tradition in the history of a particular group.

Despite these considerations, we must make some selection

of the mass of tradition and give greater emphasis to some classes than to others. It is obvious, I think, that of my four classes, two, the first, *myth*, and the third, *tribal and family traditions*, will receive the greatest attention. In a limited sense, they can be considered a continuum: the tribal traditions take place in the present social order; myths refer to the time before the establishment (or to the establishing) of the present social order. Some scholars have distinguished myth in this way and it seems a useful conceptualization (one which in fact is sometimes given by the informant who furnished the tradition).

However, the term myth has been so long and variously discussed by persons of such different nationalities, centuries, disciplines and personal interests that it remains a confusing word which we must look at more closely.

In the nineteenth century, interpretations of myth aroused great interest. Several reputations were enhanced by work on myth; today, very little of these interpretations are accepted, and if some of the names, such as Max Müller, are remembered, it is because of other accomplishments.

The Grimm brothers started out as collectors of German folktales, but with the second edition in 1819, they began to discuss the relation of their collection to collections made in other lands. From then on to 1856, the successive additions were vehicles for their theorizing. Their two major conclusions were (1) the tales were an inheritance from an Indo-European culture of antiquity and would therefore be found only in countries where Indo-European languages are spoken; and (2) that tales (Märchen) are broken-down myths. The first of these points has long been disproved; the second may sometimes be true but is not true of all tales.

This was the period of great advances in the study of the Indo-European language family, and it is understandable that some scholars would exaggerate its importance for other studies. Another of the theorists of the folktale was a linguist, Max Müller, who suggested that myths were a disease of language. Without writing, the memories of a long-dead hero would become confused, and if his name had a similarity to that of some animal, the two might become mixed to give a supernatural being of compound characteristics.

Andrew Lang punctured these balloons by showing that

myths and tales were widely diffused outside the Indo-European-speaking countries, that the same myths, often with different symbols, existed in different language areas, and that they could not be the result of confusion of language, misunderstanding of puns, or any other linguistic disease.

Another interpretation that became popular was that myths had always a hidden meaning which referred to natural phenomena, especially to the sun. Angelo de Gubernatis, for example, derived Cinderella from the aurora.[5]

Theodor Benfey and others tried to trace all folklore back to India and in the attempt to prove the case added substantially to the collections, but merely showed that India was one of a number of centres of dissemination.

Andrew Lang and E. B. Taylor helped to turn attention to the folklore of those whom it was customary, in those days, to call savage or primitive peoples. Sir James Frazer's enormous work, in which he kept in constant view the inter-relation of myth and ceremonies, was on a much more inclusive scale than that of his predecessors, but the comparative method which he used was criticized by Bronislaw Malinowski,[6] who insisted that the folklore of a given people must be studied in the context of their specific culture.

Of all the attempts to construct a theory of myth, at least three may be considered as currently contending with each other: The Myth-Ritual Theory; the Social Charter Theory; and the Iconatrophy Theory.

Robertson Smith in his *Religion of the Semites* pointed out the interplay of myth and ritual but did not formulize the idea. Arnold van Gennep[7] restricted the term myth to tales directly related to rites. Its recitation was necessary to the efficacy of the rite. It also, and other tales as well, may be important as an educating factor since duties were explained by exemplification.

The view that myth is the verbal complement of ritual has also affected its acceptability for historical studies. In an extreme position, adopted by Lord Raglan, any possibility of history is denied. In *The Hero*, Lord Raglan demonstrates that myths of heroes in various cultures have a number of common features. The myths run to a pattern because the rituals, from which they were derived, are (or were) similar, he argues, and it is hardly feasible that living individuals would have had such a similarity of experience. Furthermore, he asserts, history is impossible without literacy. He cites a case in which a French peasant, a generation or so after Napoleon, did not even know the name of the former Emperor of the French. Illiterates have no interest in history, is the lesson he draws from this. Only when events can be written down will history develop because otherwise the succeeding generations forget because they have no interest. History is a clerkly profession.

This is an extremely dubious line of reasoning. The European peasant is not necessarily typical of the people of other societies. I have shown elsewhere that peasant and tribesman are two quite different social conditions. The peasantry is only a part of a society, in which another part, the aristocracy, was more concerned with the political history. But peasants do actually have some traditions applicable to their own level of society. The Polynesians, who have a well-organized body of tradition, are farmers but they are not peasants upon whom a stultifying past of serfdom weighs. The stratification in the Polynesian society is not such that class division separates the farmers and fishermen from an interest in the history of their chiefs. It is not warranted to draw inferences about non-European peoples from the behaviour of European peasants.

Murdock, in fact, flatly rejected oral traditions in his culture history of African peoples, but made the Polynesians an exception because of the care with which their traditions are transmitted.[8] He apparently was unaware of the *griots* in West Africa and 'remembrancers' elsewhere on this continent. At any rate, it would be just as wrong to take Polynesian or *griot* tradition at face value.

The 'Functionalists' made an attack on oral traditions which denied the value for history of even the family traditions. The primary voice in this attack was that of Bronislaw Malinowski. He showed that one of the functions of traditions was to validate an individual's, or more usually a family's, position in the society. A deity or some supernatural event had disposed that things should be as they are. Such and such a person had a claim to be chief because he was a descendant of the chief or chiefly family who founded the chiefdom or of another chief who did so and so. The traditions were not history because those parts of the tradition not useful in supporting the claims of existing groups and individuals would be lost, and there was always a tendency to twist the traditions to further the interests of the group concerned. The traditions were the 'Charter of the Society'. They justified the *status quo* but they were not reliable to explain how it had come about. Radcliffe-Brown occupied a half-way house, arguing against pseudo-history but maintaining an interest in history.[9]

After an examination of some traditions in south-eastern Ghana, Ivor Wilks, in an article in *Universitas*, came to the conclusion that traditions reflect ancient diplomacy and not history. They are, he says, deceptive as history and he would not have understood the meaning of those he investigated if he had not had documents which furnished him a history of the occasion. History may illuminate traditions, he concludes, but it can hardly be the other way around. This conclusion is similar to Malinowski's that traditions give the social charter, but it is not a mere application of the older position but results from a very cogent examination of actual traditions.

Robert Graves[10] has put forward the claim that myths are sometimes stories that grow up around the religious art of a previous people which is no longer understood by the generation of myth-makers. He calls this process *iconatrophy*. He has in mind particularly, the Greeks, whom he felt found the 'Mycenaean' friezes, seals, painted pottery, and sculpture puzzling. Although this interpretation of Greek myth is plausible in some instances, it is hardly subject to demonstrable proof. However, the case of the story of Lady Godiva would seem to come closer to vindicating *iconatrophy*.

Whether this process was ever significant in Africa would be difficult to say. We have not, at the moment, a situation as favourable for utilizing it in formulating hypotheses as the Eastern Mediterranean because we have very little ancient art; but archaeology may furnish us with more, and the rock paintings may be brought into historical relation with existing peoples.

The Myth-Ritual theory is widely held by students of comparative religion (in particular of ancient Middle Eastern and Mediterranean religions), but as William Bascom pointed out, this point of view is not so common among anthropologists.[11] The Social Charter theory is common among social anthropologists but not necessarily among cultural anthropologists. The iconatrophy theory has not as yet, as far as I am aware, been adopted by anyone other than its originator, Robert Graves. It is possible that these different views are not necessarily contradictory; they may indicate the way to a typology of myths: each of the three producing a certain type of myth, although it is probable that after formation, influence from the sources may affect the content of the myth.

If a myth originated in association with a ritual, our first task would be to identify it as such. So much study has been given to this that there are now believed to be certain earmarks of (this kind of) myth. (Some would hold that this is the only kind of myth.) Then we would attempt to identify or reconstruct the ritual which would give us some information on the institutions and practices that were religiously sanctioned. This would be data for social history, but the actions of the mythological beings, in so far as their actions are the reflection of ritual, would not be historical actions, i.e. actions of deceased men. But at this point, we could ask if the myth, after its formation, had not grown through accretions; a mythological character may have become identified with a national hero or even a series of such heroes and all of the actions cannot then be explained by an attribution to ritual. When actions which are the symbolic reflections of ritual are extracted, the remainder may be treated as possibly historical and subjected to the canons of criticism applicable to this kind of tradition.

If a myth was born from the need to sanctify the structure of a society, but was not midwifed by ritual at its birth, it would be virtually impossible to show that this was so in a way that would separate it from other kinds of myths. It seems to me that a pressure exists in all societies to create a 'Social Charter', but I think this more frequently occurs through the modification of existing myth than by the creation of new ones. This, then, it seems to me, is a force for distortion rather than creation.

If a myth arose through iconatrophy, the problem would be to find the *icon* which gave rise to it. Where there is an ample art of durable material this may be accomplished satisfactorily. But when the icon no longer exists, the conclusion must remain speculative. Since the icon itself may have exemplified a rite, this type of myth could be related to the myth-ritual type, but is a step removed because the people explaining the icon had already forgotten the ritual and therefore the original meaning of the icon. We need not assume that the icon always depicted a ritual, but it perhaps frequently did because this kind of icon would be recurrent. Therefore some examples are apt to survive, whereas other kinds of icons would be more likely to be unique and stand a greater chance of perishing.

In addition, some attempts have been made by followers of Freud to explain the genesis of myth as the projection from the 'unconscious' of certain relationships which were axiomatically accepted as natural to the human condition. This has never been accepted by more than a handful of anthropologists. The Oedipus and Electra complexes are examples of these stereotypes. These suggestions have rarely found favour with anthropologists, however, and it has been shown that in a matrilineal society the pressures on the individual would be significantly different.[12] It has also been asserted that the Oedipus-type story has a wide, but limited, distribution (and that Africa is not included); this implies a cultural rather than a biological source.[13]

Myth is patently more difficult to assess than tribal and family traditions, and one must go through several steps of analysis before arriving at material that is comparable, one hopes, to the tribal traditions.

Family and tribal traditions, no less than myths, have been denied any reliance. In a bitter controversy that appeared in *American Anthropologist*, Robert Lowie declared, 'I cannot attach to oral tradition any historical value whatsoever under any conditions whatsoever'.[14]

Distortion through forgetfulness or embellishment for artistic effect or intercalations from other traditions, or innovations to explain what had become obscure, seemed too much for anthropologists to deal with.

One aspect that was not appreciated is that the possession of a sense of history is something independent of literacy, (*pace* Raglan). We can say that the literate Indians had so little sense of history that for certain periods the primary sources are the works of Chinese travellers; yet Indians were writing theological or philosophical works. On the other hand, however, the illiterate Polynesians have been often acclaimed for their sense of history.

The result of all this onslaught upon the nature and value of oral tradition is that for the last few decades there has been very little work done seriously in this field. If we are on the verge of a reversal of opinion, as I believe we are, this neglect will prove unfortunate because some traditions that could have been collected are now lost, due to the disappearance of the old ways of life under Western impact and the death of the old people who remembered the traditional lore. The remaining resources, also, are rapidly diminishing.

There is one specialized field that has been relatively little affected by the Malinowski and Raglan arguments. This is the study of Greek myths. These are traditions which have been recorded a long, long time ago, but they were for a long time previously passed down orally, and may be considered as equivalent to oral traditions more recently collected or still being, or to be, collected. But academically and professionally, Greek myths are separated from other traditions. The audience for the remarks of Lowie, Malinowski *et al.* were anthropologists concerned largely with non-literate people, but the specialists in Greek myths were, on the other hand, concerned with *literature*. Also classical studies were long established, with their own standards, and these anti-historical arguments were cushioned by a good deal of study of Greek traditions which did yield historical information.

Perhaps the most dramatic demonstration was H. Schliemann's faith in the historical validity of Homer's epic poems, which led to the excavation of Troy. His archaeological methods were somewhat too crude and have been surpassed by later refinements; so, too, his simple faith in the smallest detail of the *Iliad* would need some modification and greater sophistication. But Schliemann's work was as much a vindication of oral tradition as it was of archaeology, but although often mentioned in connexion with the history of archaeology, it is seldom brought into discussions of oral tradition.

The study and interpretation of these Greek traditions has continued unabated, and despite the fact that Greek is no longer as popular a subject in the schools as it used to be, recent

studies maintain the high standards in the quality of scholarship
that has long been established in the field of classics.

What do these studies show? Let us glean a few points from a
recent summary by Denys Page of the historical data in the *Iliad*.

Objects found archaeologically in recent times, such as the
boar's-tusk helmet and the long shield, prove the accuracy of
the Homeric description of the accessories of war. These
Mycenaean accoutrements had been long forgotten when the
Iliad was put down in writing, but the knowledge of the old
ornament had been passed down.

The long shield had particularly bothered students of Homer,
because the Greek shield was circular and it would have been
impossible for it to have hit a hero's heels as he walked with it,
to or from a battle, slung on his back. Homer's image was explained by the discovery of archaeologists, and, in a measure,
the historicity of Homer was vindicated.

The war chariot presents a slightly different aspect of the
retention of the past in the Homeric poems. The chariot itself is
adequately described, but Homer obviously did not understand how the chariot was used in warfare. He had the heroes
ride up to the battlefield and then dismount to fight! The
chariot had gone out of use with the introduction of more
manœuvrable cavalry and had not been used for a long time
previous to the final development of the *Iliad*.[15]

How it comes about that the tradition is more accurate in
some respects than in others can be explained by the method of
composition of the poems. A professional group of bards had
gradually built up a common fund of idioms and formular
phrases useful in eulogizing the military exploits of their
patrons or of the patron's ancestors. This method of composing
an original poem, in perfect metrical form, from a stock of
traditional formular phrases, has been found to exist in modern
times in the Balkans not far from where the *Iliad* was composed.

Thus it seems that bards, travelling from court to court, had
to learn the stories of the various participants in the Trojan
War. As long as there were direct descendants, who would
know the story of their ancestors' exploits but want to hear
them sung again, there would be a protest against deletion of
any laudatory detail but no protest, probably, to elaboration of
the glorious story; and so inventions of divine help had free

rein. Finally, when the very nature of the society had changed and the bards were no longer singing for the families of the *personae dramatis* but for a public less intimately concerned, the individual stories were combined to make the epic that we know.

Obsolete words, like πόντος and ἁλός would continue to be employed because they were embedded in the formular phrases, even though no longer familiar to the listeners. Whole stanzas probably came down intact, and in this way descriptions of past events and no longer familiar objects survived. Thus the work is not a history, but material that must be analysed by an historian.

How much history do we get from the *Iliad*? The war itself, which many had doubted, can be taken as an actual happening. Again this is validated by archaeology. We know which cities of the Achaeans were involved and perhaps the names of some of the leaders. We know something, as we have seen, of their military equipment. Not a great deal more. This is not a history to be compared with the history of Thucydides of a later war.

This may not seem much, but it is only one tradition and there are a host of others. The other 'Homeric' epic, the *Odyssey*, now believed to have been composed by someone else and about two centuries later than the *Iliad*, indicates the exploration of the central and western Mediterranean before the foundation there of Greek colonies. The Voyage of the Argonauts also indicates early, probably earlier, maritime expansion and trade. Theseus and the Minotaur seems to refer to a Greek-speaking people's conflict with the Minoan thalassocracy, and possibly the one which resulted in the establishment of the language of the 'Linear B' script on Crete. The Hercules cycle, in part a diffusion of a Western Asian myth, has grafted upon it some of the exploits of the Dorians in their contest against their predecessors in Hellas.

The whole body of Greek mythology has been compiled into a dictionary by Robert Graves. He gives the various versions of each story and notes the sources of each version. Each story is followed by an explanatory and interpretive section. Unfortunately, the commentaries are not accompanied by any references to 'today's archaeological and anthropological knowledge', in the light of which, the flyleaf tells us, the commentaries were made. In this a good deal of speculative history is suggested, some of which is quite controversial. This is quite a different kettle of fish from the above-noted work of Denys Page, in which every step is attested by full documentation. To many readers, indeed, Graves may exemplify the dangers of attempting to use traditions historically, and his interpretations have not, as yet at least, won wide acceptance. His general theory is set forth in *The White Goddess*. The work that he has done earns him a place of significance in the study of myth, but the cavalier fashion in which he asserts his interpretations without citing his alleged archaeological and anthropological data increases the difficulty of using *The Greek Myths*; and *The White Goddess* is so dense and obscurantist in places that one reader told me that it had obviously been meant to be taken as a spoof. Indeed, one can see a similarity to the satiric treatment Norman Douglass gives his character 'Monsignor Parrelli, the learned and genial historian of Nepenthe' in *South Wind*.

If it is possible to give widely different interpretations to traditions, and if the best guide to reliability is archaeology, one may ask, 'Of what use then are oral traditions? Can't one get as much information from archaeology alone?' Archaeology had also demonstrated how much the traditions have not preserved. There is no mention in the *Iliad* of the extensive bureaucracy of Crete and Pylos indicated by the decipherment of the Linear B tablets.

To recognize the limitations of the use of traditions is not the same as denying their value. Thus far, their use has been most exploited by the archaeologist, not only in finding a site, as in Schliemann's case, mentioned earlier, but also in reconstructing the social context in which the exhumed artifacts were used.

A somewhat different but analogous case is that of the Bible. Nelson Glueck says:

The Bible, of course, is essentially a theological document . . . It is only secondarily a book of history and geography. Selected historical materials were incorporated into the Biblical text for the sole purpose of illustrating the kind of religious teaching . . .

But, he insists, 'Historians, nevertheless, and archeologists in particular have learned to rely upon the amazing accuracy of historical memory in the Bible'. He then tells how clues in various biblical passages, when put together with an historian's reasoning, led to the discovery in Negheb of the City of Copper and the Valley of the Smiths.[16] One could easily multiply such testimonies to the usefulness of the Bible to archaeology.

Some may object that the Bible and/or Greek myths are not in the same class as the traditions of non-literate societies. It must be admitted that they are more ancient, because recorded long ago; but as traditions they are fundamentally analogous.

The fact is that wherever archaeologists work, they are assiduous in their attention to local traditions.

Well, we have talked at some length about examples from the lands around the eastern Mediterranean, but does there actually exist anything comparable south of the Sahara? Something that has only recently been put down in print, I offer as a West African analogue to the *Iliad*. Balla Fasseké, a Malinké griot, is the counterpart of Homer, the Greek bard, and the wrath of Soundiata rather than the wrath of Achilles is the focus of the story. This has been published by *Présence Africaine* and T. D. Niane, who is not the author but the collector and translator (into French) of the tradition.[17] He tells us in the preface that the man from whom he heard the tale is a descendant of Balla Fasseké and that Balla Fasseké was the personal griot and companion of Soundiata. Now, seven centuries is a long time for this story to have been transmitted orally, perhaps some twenty generations, but it is about comparable to Homer's distance from the events he sang about. In one respect the tradition of Soundiata may have been more fortunate than that of the Trojan War, because there has been less social change in the Sudan in these seven centuries. Soundiata was early in the Islamic period and the kind of society he knew persisted (despite an eventual decline in the fortunes of his successors and a rise in the fortunes of some of his neighbours) until the relatively recent French intrusion; whereas in the seven centuries separating Homer from Mycaenae and Troy, the Achaean society (as he called it, Mycenaean as archaeologists term it) gave way to a quite different, though related, culture, that of the Hellenes. It is possible, therefore, that historically the Malinké epic is sounder than the Greek one because it was not transmitted through a period of cultural change. It is especially likely to be sound if the modern teller of the tale has it in unbroken succession to Balla Fasseké.

The historical elements in the story are the exile of Soundiata, the war against Sumanguro, the defection of the Sosso's nephew to Soundiata, and the settlement of territory and power after the victory which is especially referred to as The Partition of the World.

There are also, as might be expected, supernatural elements in the story: the prodigious prowess of Soundiata; the sorcery of Sumanguru; the ritual sacrifice of livestock for victory.

The recording of this tradition is a valuable contribution to the study of the West African past. Strangely enough, the editors of the *Tarikh el-Fettach*, half a century ago, knew of traditions of Soundiata current in the Sudan but this did not lead to the recording of them.

A. Kagame has recorded the dynastic poetry and genea-logies of Rwanda.[18] This kingdom has a wealth of traditions, as J. Roscoe had long ago shown that some neighbouring Uganda kingdoms have. More recent collecting among the latter peoples has been done by Roland Oliver.[19]

The C.M.S. Bookshop in Lagos in 1934 published Chief Jacob V. Egharevbas's *A Short History of Benin*. This was a selection of the oral traditions of the Benin Kingdom, and was an interesting example of an African setting down the tradi-tions of his own people. It had some shortcomings in that it was incomplete, there was no indication of the existence of variant versions, and we were given little information on the sources of the printed version. Also, at points, interpolations were made of extraneous matter from European sources, which was permis-sible, especially as Egharevba thought of his work as finished narrative history. These interpolations have no place in the body of the oral traditions, and in the publishing of a collection as documents for further historical analysis would properly have a place only in footnotes.

The weaknesses of the work were far outweighed by the intrinsic worth of the material, and Egharevba, while writing many other booklets on his people, reprinted his *Short History* in 1953. In 1960, a third edition with additions in several chapters, was brought out by the Ibadan University Press. We would certainly like to see many more individuals in Africa with interest, initiative, and judgement comparable to Chief Egharevba.

Odú, a journal of Yoruba studies, has featured articles on oral traditions.

Ian Cunnison, further south in Africa, collected traditions in the Luapula valley.[20] He found that there were only family, or lineage, traditions and that to get an historical overview of the whole people he had to put them together in a synthesis of his own formulation because the people there had not been interested in that level of abstraction.

Jan Vansina, among a more historically minded people in the Congo basin, recorded the traditions of the Bakuba and found them to be extensive and organized.[21]

The contributions of these workers is an indication of the palpable resurgence of interest in oral tradition. In addition to those mentioned above, there are projects in Nigeria and Rhodesia, connected with a university in each case, in which oral traditions are included in an historical research scheme. A Commission for Technical Co-operation in Africa South of the Sahara conference at Bukavu recommended the collection of oral traditions throughout Africa. The International African Institute held a seminar on Ethno-History in Dakar at which oral traditions were prominently featured. It might be counted a small part of this resurgence that at a meeting of the Historical Society of Ghana, I presented a paper on the traditions of the foundation of Sijilmassa.[22]

A fine example of a way to go about collecting oral traditions was given right here at the University College of Ghana when David Tait, an anthropologist, and John Fage, an historian, set up a plan for the recording and interpretation of Konkomba traditions. This was brought to an end by the unfortunate death of David Tait.[23]

Some horrible examples can be given of how *not* to record traditions. Most pertinent in Ghana is the instance of Mrs. Meyerowitz.[24] One can but admire her energy, persistence and interest, but unfortunately her methods of work leave much to be desired. No one can independently check her work as we ought to be able to do. If she had deposited in some archive or library a copy of the actual traditions of the Akan then it would be possible to obtain a critical evaluation of her interpretation of the traditions, but she has not made the traditions themselves available. Indeed it is not clear that she ever recorded them but seems merely to have made notes of those things that interested her; in which case even her notes would be of little value because the items are out of context. In addition, she has made faulty use of linguistics.

I am not saying that her thesis is wrong, but only that she has worked in such a way that we cannot check the steps of her work.

If there is some excuse for an amateur making use of such faulty methodology, there is none for a professional anthropologist. M. J. Herskovits, whose teacher, Franz Boas, explicitly laid down the still-accepted rules for recording traditions, was incredibly careless or naïve or both when he collected the traditions recently published as *Dahomean Narrative*.[25] The stories were told in Fon and a local translator turned them into French. Herskovits recorded them in English and obtained neither the original nor the first translation! Bleek had long since set the standard on the continent with his publication of Bushman tales in the original and English, and Rattray had dealt with a comparable difficulty of three versions when he presented Hausa in Arabic script, Hausa in Latin script, and English.

The recorder of oral traditions should start with the teller of the tales. What is his position in the society? What groups does he belong to and what positions or titles does he have?

All variant versions, in so far as possible, should also be recorded, and then the information on the social status of each teller may prove to be significant in understanding the variations which may represent group interests in some instances.

The tradition itself should be put down verbatim and here a tape recorder is advantageous because the teller does not have to be interrupted. Durable, lightweight, portable, shoulder-slung, quality fidelity recorders are today available but expensive. When the tale is chanted or told in a highly formalized manner, interruptions can be disconcerting to the teller and perhaps result in a condensed or truncated version being given. The first translation should be a literal one, taking each vocable as it appears in the original. Then this may be put into idiomatic English.

The document has now been produced.

The cross-examination of the tradition can now begin. This will involve:

an analysis of the formular elements, if any;

a linguistic scrutiny of the language employed, especially of archaisms;

a comparison of the various versions of the tradition;

a comparison of the tradition with the rest of the oral tradition of the people;

a comparison of the tradition with traditions of other people;

an attempt to correlate items in the tradition with ethnographic data;

an attempt to correlate items in the tradition with written documents, if any.

This is the exegesis of the document; the production of commentaries (equivalent to the scholiasts of the classicist or the glosses of the historian).

We know that the traditions of Benin refer to the Yoruba, and those of the Hausa to Bornu. One can sometimes check the other. Herodotus was aware of convergences in the traditions of different groups. He informs us, for example, 'Such is the account the Theraeans give. In the sequel of the history their accounts tally with those of the people of Cyrene . . .'[26]

Very few traditions are so thoroughly examined; in many cases, one or more of the categories of relevant materials may be lacking or scanty, but the examination should be carried as far as practical. The most common fault is the telescoping of several steps, which results in obscuring the actual tradition and confusing interpretation and tradition so that other scholars are unable to judge the exact content of the tradition.

How far back can we hope to go by means of oral traditions? In many instances, only a few generations; in others, several centuries, perhaps in fortunate circumstances even somewhat beyond a millennium, but this would be unusual. However, traditions formerly recorded, usually imperfectly and incompletely, can be used. There are versions of certain African traditions which were put down in various European languages from the time of the Portuguese expansion to the present. In Arabic for certain regions, they go back a good deal earlier.

One point, though relatively well known, bears repeating.

Eclipses are likely to be mentioned in the traditions and since these can be dated, the associated persons and events can be put into a very precise chronological period. The first instance noted in Africa was by Emil Torday among the Bushongo. This same eclipse, we now realize, was noted by three different peoples and recorded in their traditions. Other instances have been found in East Africa and Dahomey.

How good is the retention of oral traditions? Naturally, this varies considerably according to the nature of the traditions and of the society possessing them as well as the manner of their transmission (whether they are the responsibility of a special class of remembrancers; are recounted in set form; associated with mnemonic devices or not; etc.) One test would be an instance where a tradition had been recorded some centuries ago and the tradition, continuing (uninfluenced by this recording) to a later date, is then again recorded and a comparison of the two should show the stability of the particular tradition. We have a few such instances but it may be questioned whether the old recording was carefully done—or at any rate comparable with the modern recording.

A somewhat different, but related, case is that of traditions, once recorded, being re-copied over the centuries. In Egypt's favourable climatic conditions, papyri on which portions of the *Iliad* had been written (in Greek) have in recent times been found. They represent the oldest version of the poem extant. The next oldest is a Byzantine copy. The difference in age is several centuries. For some fragments the concordance is virtually complete; but for others we are dealing with collateral traditions.

The danger of careless recording is now increased by the growth of literacy because after a few years the recorded, but inaccurate, version is quoted to subsequent investigators. Many Ga and Akwapim elders are not only familiar with Rheindorf's book but take it as their source. Rheindorf may or may not be accurate; he was a scholar of his time, and oral traditions were then not usual materials. At any rate, it would be difficult to check on him now. Some of the recently published traditions by authors less familiar with the peoples than was Rheindorf and not as careful scholars as he was, are a threat to later workers in the area because these books may become standard.

A good deal more discussion is needed on the proper assessment of oral traditions, and this will probably come since there has been a return of interest in recent years.

Jan Vansina has emerged as undoubtedly the most knowledgeable and cogent of the proponents of the historicity of oral traditions, and the one who has written in greatest detail on the problems involved in the collection, analysis and interpretation of traditions. He has not given as important a place to myth as we have in this discussion, but no worker in this field can afford to be unfamiliar with his writings on tribal traditions. No one person as yet has done for myth what Vansina has done for tribal traditions.

Malinowski was right that traditions, or at least some traditions, are the social charter, but this does not eliminate their usefulness for history. He was also correct that traditions are subject to distortion, but if we were to throw out everything subject to distortion historians would have few documents of any kind. The task is to find out how to detect distortion. It is also true that some traditions arose from ritual, but if we can reconstruct the meaning of the ritual we will have achieved an increase in historical understanding. In any case, the ritual, where it has been the source of the original form, is usually not the only level of meaning because there may well be other elements encrusted upon the myth. Most importantly, some traditions are basically historical and are the property of people with a sense of history.

We can conclude with Samuel Johnson's caustic comment: 'History is what is recorded by contemporaries; all else is romance', and note that Balla Fasseké was a contemporary of Soundiata, and in the broad sense of the term *record* suggested in Chapter One, the tradition of Soundiata would meet Johnson's criteria. The heritage of the ears gives us evidence to be submitted to the canons of criticism. The data which comes from this process will be an important part of the eventual synthesis of pre-literary history.

> The whole of social and linguistic life, the changes in population, the reconstruction of their economic history and cultural relations, may be deduced from linguistic history.
>
> *Antonio Tovar*

CHAPTER FOUR

HISTORY IN LANGUAGE

ALMOST everyone will have been aware of the fact that archaeology and oral traditions were somehow related to history, but there are two other fields, just as intimately connected with history, that are not so well known in this respect except to initiates. Of these two, ethnology and linguistics, the former is perhaps more widely known for its historical connexion; but following the practice of starting with the one with the more developed methodology and greater reliability (already employed in setting the order of discussion in the preceding chapters) we will have to take linguistics first. Not only is there greater precision of technique in linguistics, but as A. L. Kroeber, who spent a good part of his life searching for cultural laws, sadly admitted, the only part of man's culture in which regularities (worthy of being dignified as laws) have been found is in language.

E. Sapir also put the study of language and culture in a relationship indicating the greater precision of the former. He wrote,

language gives us a sort of stratified matrix to work in for the purposes of unraveling culture sequences; its relation to culture history may be roughly compared—one should not press the analogy—to that of geology to paleontology.

To give the context of this comparison, Sapir's preceding words are:

language, like culture, is a composite of elements of very different age, some of its features reaching back into the mists of an impenetrable

past, others being the product of a development or need of yesterday. If now we succeed in putting the changing face of culture into relation with the changing face of language we shall have obtained a measure, vague or precise according to the specific circumstances, of the relative ages of the culture elements.[1]

Linguistics, thus, is not a thing separate from the study of culture but is a part of the whole and is so treated in departments of anthropology in American universities. Language, however, is the part of culture that has thus far been most amenable to study by scientific techniques.

The study of language is about as old as that of history; both go back, in the Western tradition, to the Greeks (although in India it is antedated by Panini's study of Sanskrit grammar). It is many centuries since then and both language study and history have developed considerably, and in doing so have come into closer relation to each other. History has become much more complex, including in its scope many more aspects of society, and at the same time has become more rigorous in its standards. In its use of an increasing variety of materials as its source data, history has learned to prefer what Marc Bloch called 'unconscious evidence', and linguistic evidence is in this category *par excellence*.

Language study has undergone three phases of development. The first was Grammar, developed by the Greeks; the second, Philology, the product of the Renaissance; and the third, Linguistics (also called in its early days, Comparative Grammar or Comparative Philology), begun in the eighteenth century. History and language study began to approach each other fairly closely in the second phase. With the appearance of linguistics it was immediately viewed as undeniably an historical study. So much so, that F. de Saussure, who was not happy with this historical preoccupation, wrote:

Since modern linguistics existed, one could say that it has been entirely absorbed in diachrony. Comparative grammar of Indo-European utilized the data it had in hand for the hypothetical reconstruction of a type of antecedent language; comparison was for it [linguistics] only a means of reconstructing the past.[2]

Saussure wanted to turn attention to structural and functional problems of linguistics, and did in fact succeed in doing so, but only at the cost, as André Martinet points out, of destroying the unity of the discipline. The study of structural aspects of linguistics can only be helpful to the historical applications of the discipline, but the 'lost unity' has had some disadvantageous effects on historical studies which we will come back to later.

The division of interests among linguists has not in any way eliminated the historical side of linguistics, for as Joseph Greenberg has pointed out, 'Unlike some other aspects of anthropology affected by the functionalist attack on history, the validity and fruitfulness of the historic approach in linguistics has never been seriously questioned.'[3]

The early work in linguistics was done on written languages and primarily in Indo-European and Semitic languages. This concentration has not yet been replaced by a more balanced distribution; at an international conference of linguists not long ago, ninety per cent. of the delegates were Indo-Europeanists. This is despite the fact that the documentation of unwritten languages began in the Age of Discovery. A short vocabulary would be collected or if an ambitious work was attempted, it was usually to translate the *Pater Noster* into the newly discovered language. In 1555, Conrad Gesner published what are probably the earliest of such translations. In 1575, André Thevet's *Cosmographie universelle* extended the number and so did Claude Duret's *Trésor de l'histoire des langues* of 1613. By 1878–89, 248 languages were so recorded in *Linguarum totius orbis vocabularia comparative Augustissimae cura collecta*. But only the second edition included American and African languages. By 1954, the British and Foreign Bible Society was able to list 836 translations of the Bible, or parts of it. In Arabic, there are a few limited vocabularies older than these in Latin script. And there is material in Nubian from the thirteenth century.

For over a century, some scientific work has been done on scattered unwritten languages. Thomas Jefferson encouraged such study of American Indian languages. But the number of languages in the world is such that it dwarfs the number of linguists. In Africa alone there are about 800 languages.

The centre of gravity continuing to remain in Indo-European studies has two results, both to be lamented: firstly that we have not progressed with the recording and analysis of non-Indo-European languages; and secondly, many linguists of the older tradition continue to regard unwritten languages as falling into a distinctly different category in regard to the operations which linguists may perform upon them. Many linguists believed—and some still do—that unwritten languages cannot yield historical data. Vendrys, Boas, Martinet and Tovar are on record for such opinions.

Despite these sceptics, a number of Proto languages have been reconstructed for families in which no member has an old written form. Greenberg had commented on this situation:

In spite of the fruitfulness of the Indo-European hypothesis and the further successes of similar hypotheses in establishing the Finno-Ugaric, Semitic, and other families, the assumptions on the bases of which these first victories of linguistics as a science were obtained were never clearly formulated, and the extension of these methods to other areas of the world has suffered from the beginning from a lack of clarity regarding the criteria of genetic relationships, resulting, in almost every major area, in a welter of conflicting classifications and even in widespread doubt as to the feasibility of any interpretation of linguistic similarities in terms of historical connections.[4]

We can no longer doubt that the genetic relationships of unwritten languages can be proved. The initial identification of Indo-European as a language family was made on descriptive material no better than what exists for many unwritten languages, though the place of certain languages will remain questionable until fuller data is available. The successes that have been obtained with unwritten languages, Proto Central Algonkian, Proto Malayo-Polynesian, and Proto Bantu, Greenburg cautions us, are more in the order of Proto-Germanic than of Proto-Indo-European, but they are earnests of further success.

There are, in fact, three procedures for the establishment of the history of a language and whether or not the language has been written is important for only one of them. These procedures are: (1) comparison of related languages; (2) comparison of documented stages of a language; and (3) internal reconstruction. The first was the original procedure and is possible with unwritten languages as long as they are recorded. The second is dependent on having old records, and although not completely eliminated in Africa, has a restricted scope there. The third procedure, internal reconstruction, was first used successfully in cases of the second type, but it is possible to extend this method to unwritten languages. Borgstron suggests:

A diachronic justification of internal reconstruction lies in the observation that some complicated patterns, particularly morphemic interchanges and certain allomorphs, have developed from simpler patterns of earlier periods . . . It is therefore legitimate to ask for such explanations of complicated patterns even in languages whose history is not known, and to obtain them by assuming that certain phonemic and morphemic changes have taken place. The changes assumed must not contradict the principles of diachronic phonetics, phonemics, or morphemics.[5]

Furthermore, he argues that alteration of one part of a linguistic system may have effects upon other parts of the system and therefore the reconstruction of one part of an earlier system may lead to further conclusions about the structure of the earlier system.

If this seems to get out of touch with reality, there are actually means of keeping the reasoning within bounds. 'The internal reconstruction is done within a single language and thus may be checked by reference to the family of which it is a member.'[6]

Some linguists are critical of such procedures, and Bazell, for example, seems to argue that they should be abolished. He asserts:

The word *induce*, still so normal in historical grammar, is sparingly used by phonemicists . . . One might recognize this and . . . draw (the) conclusion: *Not* that the notion is essential to synchronic linguistics, but that it would be better dispensed with in historical linguistics.[7]

If we don't go as far as Bazell, at least we must recognize that internal reconstruction in unwritten languages must be used with every caution. And if carefully used, internal reconstruction can help to overcome the disadvantage of not having more documented stages.

Genetic relationships are not by any means the only historical problems of linguistics. For example, contact between speakers of different languages, which usually leads to some borrowing, does not result in a confusion of the genetic relationships, but can yield useful information on culture contact. But the fact is that the lack of an accepted genetic classification is a handicap for most other historico-linguistic research. If not exactly a *sine qua non*, it is something urgently to be desired for any historical perspective.

Attempts have been made over the years to discern the language families of Africa. Meinhof, Werner, Homberger and Westermann have suggested classifications. For just over a decade, the classification which has occupied the centre of attention is that of Greenberg. It is accepted in its general out- lines without demur by other American linguists and seems to have had a quite extensive acceptance on the continent of Europe, but is generally rejected by British linguists.

One objection is that this classification has not yet resulted in the elucidation of regularities similar to 'Grimm's law' (for certain patterns of sound changes in the Indo-European language family), and that to demonstrate the presence or absence of these regularities requires further analysis, some of which would be dependent on the collection of more complete descriptive data. Thus this criticism cannot be definitive unless and until it is established that it is *impossible* to derive such correspondences from this classification.

One is tempted to ask if this disagreement is deeper than the immediate issue, if it is not due to a difference in orientation, if, in other words, it is not, in some measure, due to the previously mentioned 'lost unity of linguistics'?

If that be the case, the 'lost unity of linguistics' may be more of a handicap to historians than to linguists in Africa, for the lack of consensus on a classification of African languages must be disconcerting to historians who want to use such a classifica- tion. In this case the lack of agreement is particularly disturbing because British linguists constitute an important part of the language specialists who have given attention to African languages and whose talents will not be directed to any work useful to historians until these linguists have some classification acceptable to them.

The linguists can go on working on non-historical problems

and be less disturbed by the failure of their colleagues to arrive at a consensus; but the historian, in so far as his work touches language, is stymied if he has no classification. What he asks from the linguists is a reasonable degree of agreement upon an existing classification—or if this is impossible, serious attempts to achieve an improved classification. There has not been much evidence of such work on classification by the critics, and so it is not surprising that some historians are using Greenberg's classification, even if they may consider it only *faute de mieux*. The results obtained by a number of linguists who do accept this classification and are carrying out further linguistic work upon this basis will also be welcomed by historians.

What we are aiming for is to accomplish for Africa something comparable to the historical inferences drawn from Proto-Indo-European. We can now say in what area the speakers of the Proto language lived. It used to be thought, on the basis of distribution of the sub-groups of Indo-European, that this was somewhere near the Caspian Sea; but now, after study of the starred-forms which indicate environment, it is believed that the homeland was near the Baltic Sea. We know what domesticated animals they had and what the material culture was like, and we can make some 'educated guesses' about their social organization.

We can already do something like this for Proto-Bantu. The Proto-Bantu speakers lived in an ecological setting in which the *elephant* and *antelope*, the *baobob* and *palm*, and the *grey parrot* were to be found. Apparently, an open forest. They cultivated these cereals: *millet*, *sorghum* and *rice* and they also grew (Bambara) *groundnuts*, *beans*, *melons*, *pumpkins* and *bananas*. They had *cattle*, *sheep*, *goats*, *chicken* and the *dog*. They used *iron*, *hoes*, *adzes*, *knives*, *spears*, *bows* and *canoes*. They wore *clothes*, put *salt* on their food, and drank *beer*. They used *cowrie shells* but whether as decoration or as currency we cannot say, but it suggests trade in either case. They were governed by *chiefs* and ministered to by *diviners*. This is on the basis of W. Bourquin's *Neue Ur-Bantu-Wortstämme*.[8] Joseph Greenberg comments that Bourquin relies too heavily on languages in the eastern division of Bantu and some revision will be necessary. Malcolm Guthrie promises soon to publish 2,500 starred forms which should extend our vista considerably.

We should be able to do this for every level of a genetic classification: for a single language, for each sub-grouping, and for
the language family itself, and for a phylum, if known to exist.

The larger the number of starred forms that can be established, the larger the number of historical deductions is likely
to be. Many of the lexical forms used to prove genetic relationships are of no use to us for history. As Sapir pointed out, we
don't need to learn that a particular people at some remote time
had *hands* and knew how *to eat*. As historians, we are interested
in culture words. Did they have *horses*, or *iron*, or *chiefs* or know
how *to tax* or *to make obeisance*. We must look beyond the short
lists cited in classifications to the full inventory of common
forms and extract every item of cultural significance.

In dealing with cognates in most African languages, attention must be given to tone. The toneme is as important as the
phoneme but is often ignored. Some internal reconstruction
done in Chinese, where it was found that a certain tone was the
sign that a final sound had been lost, might be a model for
Africanist research.

Sapir also pointed out, in his seminal article, 'Time Perspective' which everyone who reads this book should study,
that the relative ages of culture items can be indicated by
linguistic data. An efflorescence of terms indicates age, as does
the use of archaic or obsolete roots or inflections. Morris
Swadish, a student of Sapir's, has put forward a method which
is claimed to be absolute, rather than relative, in its dating, but
consideration of this system will be left to the chapter on
chronology.

Areal relationships as well as the genetic can also be eluci-
dated. Convergence of phonology, and/or borrowing of tone or
clicks or unusual combinations like the velar kp or gb may
indicate a period of contact. (However, note Darlington's
physiologic explanation, cf. e.g. F. Bresnahan.) The dispersion
of idioms through unrelated languages, like the widespread
metaphoric uses of the verb 'to eat' in Africa are important to
note. But for cultural content, none are as important as loan
words. If a word can be established as a starred form in one
language family (or subdivision thereof) and cognates appear
in some languages belonging to another family a case of borrowing is indicated. If the history of sound shifts within the

families concerned is known, it can even be established at what time, in relation to these shifts, the borrowing was done. Thus the actual cultural content of the borrowing, the direction and extent of diffusion, and a relative time can be recovered by linguistic analysis.

Place names can yield a good deal of historical inferences, but onomastics is apt to be tricky and particularly where an assumption of a 'sub-stratum' is made (i.e. that the place name comes from a previous and usually little-known language) the results are more often than not controversial.

There is great promise in linguistics for African history, but there are problems as well with its use. One problem, already referred to as the 'lost unity', has been noted. Another is the paucity of linguists and the number of non-historical linguistic problems with which they tend to be preoccupied. But even if linguists could feed us with data as fast as historians could use it, there would still be problems involved in its use. We must remember that linguistics is not an infallible historical guide. Inferences have been made on European languages that had to be rejected because other historical materials refuted them.

Sapir gave us this caution:

I do not consider any single one of the inferential criteria . . . as necessarily valid in a specific case. An argument . . . may be entirely convincing in the handling of one problem, yet appear far-fetched or even totally inapplicable in the handling of another. Everything depends upon the specific conditions of a given problem. And needless to say, any one criteria is never to be applied to the exclusion of, or in opposition to, all others.[9]

With these limitations in mind, I offer a corollary to T. Mommsen's advice to historians to study language,[10] and suggest that African historians study linguistics.

A detailed study of customs in their relation to the total culture of the tribe practising them, in connection with an investigation of their geographical distribution among neighbouring tribes, affords us almost always a means of determining with considerable accuracy the historical causes that led to the formation of the customs in question and to the psychological processes that were at work in their development.

Franz Boas

CHAPTER FIVE

THE STUDY OF MANKIND

HERODOTUS has been dubbed 'The Father of Ethnology' in addition to his well-known paternity of history. And the offspring do have some fraternal resemblances.

Herodotus described the customs of the various peoples of his day whom he visited. He was surprised at, and failed to understand, matrilineal customs, as so many after him have done. He was amused at the barbarians beyond Greece who were shocked at nudity (as some of them still are) and concluded that a calm acceptance of nudity, no less than an appreciation of beauty of form, was a sign of a civilized person.[1]

Tacitus and some other classical authors would also qualify as early ethnologists in this sense. Marco Polo was a most important one for Europe in a later period, although he did not travel as far or write as extensively as some Arabic travellers, in particular Ibn Battuta.

The Age of Discovery naturally resulted in an extension of ethnographic knowledge—and speculation. As J. L. Myers has shown, the thought-provoking discovery of strange customs had an important stimulating and revolutionary effect on European political philosophy. At that time there was no division of political thought from the other social sciences; it was all under the rubric of 'Moral' philosophy. John Locke knew only about the New England Indians, whereas Jean-Jacques Rousseau knew only of the Caribbean Indians, and this may to some extent have contributed to the differences in their thought. The

chance selection of customs reported and the partiality of the reporter might also have been a factor, as well as the temperament and experience of the thinker; but in any case, the new knowledge of the embryonic ethnology gave fresh and varied models with which to compare European experience.

Careful comparative study of customs did not come, however, until the nineteenth century, with the work of Bastian, Tylor, and Morgan. By this time the 'Idea of Progress' and Darwin's concepts began to affect the intellectual atmosphere, so that ethnology as a modern discipline was developed in a period that was almost obsessed with evolutionism. It is natural that its early concern was with the origin of institutions and their social evolution.

It is undeniable that institutions did have an origin and that they did develop through a series of modifications; but the means then available of perceiving these lines of societal growth were not as successful as the means available for discovering the sequence of biological forms. Some claims of culture history were on shaky foundations, or over-extended, or sometimes downright naïve. A reaction was sure to come, and it did, but instead of having the effect of stimulating a search for better methods of historical study, the reaction turned attention generally to a different type of study, and functionalism ruled the day.

E. B. Tylor's study of the origin of religion has been criticized for not allowing for the non-rational motivations of man.

L. H. Morgan's study of the origin of the family has been criticized for making unwarranted deductions from the terminology of classificatory kinship systems, and for seeming to imply a single, unilinear, obligatory line of evolution through a series of stages that had definitive criteria of a type different in one case from that of the others. But perhaps Morgan's greatest burden was to be adopted by Karl Marx and F. Engels, the latter incorporating Morgan's system into his *Family, State, and Private Property*. Morgan's theory has been ever since, and is today, the official Communist doctrine. Anti-communist feeling, or the fear of being mistaken for a communist, have made it difficult to retrieve even what is valid from his *Ancient Society*; it is ignored that Morgan himself was a staunch capitalist.

Elliott Smith's 'Heliolithic theory' has completely collapsed.

He claimed that all civilization had been diffused from Egypt. This was too simplistic an idea and the mechanics and chronology of diffusion became too involved for credibility, although echoes of the theory are sometimes still heard in Africa.

Graebner's *Kulturkreis* theory, which was a more reasonable diffusion theory than Smith's, came to grief when archaeology contradicted some of its claims and the proponents withdrew the theory. This theory was never influential in the English-speaking world, but was widely espoused on the European continent, particularly in the Germanic countries. Writings by Germans of this school on Africa are fairly extensive, and still worthy of study for their data on African societies, their traditions, art and customs, even if we must today reject the theoretical framework of the works. The Germans have not given up their historical orientation but have turned to a search for a new guide.

The collapse of the theories which had been promulgated in the English-speaking world, however, left a wreckage that discouraged nearly all of the British and most of the American anthropologists for a long time from attempting new historical interpretations. Among those who continued to pursue historical studies were A. L. Kroeber, who lived through this period of dispute to become accepted as the doyen of American anthropology, and could say towards the end of his long life of scholarship that he considered anthropology more an historical than a scientific study.

V. Gordon Childe's books are undoubtedly the best known of the current 'schools', if they may be called such, of culture history; but his work, unlike most others, is strongly based on archaeology.[2]

Leslie White proposes a 'culturology' that courageously salvages some of Morgan's ideas to which he adds a cultural determinism that has attracted few adherents.[3]

Julian Steward also has attempted to explain the process of Cultural Evolution. There has been a partial recovery by now, and there seems to be a good deal more interest in recent years in culture history, particularly by younger cultural anthropologists.

However, the attention has turned away, in some measure, from grandiose, over-all schemes to more limited and localized historical studies. This shift of emphasis makes it more like history and less like the philosophy of history. This distinction was not commonly made in earlier studies, and the distinction between evolution and history was left vague. Marshall Sahlins has now made a distinction between general evolution and specific evolution; the former being the succession of stages, and the latter the sequence of developments within a single grouping.

Ethno-history, in the early use of the word, meant the use of archival materials in the service of ethnography. The history of a tribe rather than the history of Man is the aim of ethno-history. That the history of Man should have been considered possible before the histories of many and varied tribes had been obtained now seems incredible.

Charles Edward Fuller's study of Gwamba in south-east Africa is an example of the use of documents in the history of a tribe or people.

When documents exist for the earlier periods of contact, it is possible to exploit them in two different ways, each of which has its value. One way is to derive from them a history of European activities in the area: a history of the expansion of European trade; of the establishment of a particular religious mission and the activities of its members; the early days of a settlement of Europeans on the African continent; the series of events by which a 'sphere of influence' became recognized and how this was later transformed into a colony or protectorate. The other way is to attempt to discover histories of the African peoples with whom the Europeans had contacts at this time.

Histories of various types and phases of European activities have for some time been making their appearance. The historian, who has generally been a European, has little difficulty in putting the data from the records in a familiar context. But a history of an African people is more difficult, the data from the writings of the Europeans has to be put in a context of the culture of that people and this can only be done in conjunction with an ethnographic study. For this reason (and for others as well) most historians have thought it outside their province, or found the difficulties too great.

We need to have a greater development of what has been dubbed ethno-history, and one way of encouraging this would be to discard the hyphenated term. Ethnologists coined it to give themselves an excuse for using the archival techniques of the historian, but it is nothing more nor less than history. The term, however, becomes an obstacle in our highly organized academic institutions. It does not 'look' like history in a college bulletin, and tends to be neglected or even actively discouraged. There is an excellent reason why historians should take a more active hand in the use of written records in the production of histories of African peoples: they have more experience in handling this kind of material, and are apt to treat it more exhaustively than an ethnographer. The latter may too soon decide he has enough background and turn back to his primary concern, his field study of the living people. This kind of history could perhaps best be pursued by an historian and an ethnographer in co-operation.

When written documents are scarce and scattered, they present special difficulties, but these difficulties have already been faced and they are not insurmountable.

Statisticians have discovered that when they have a small number of items in a class that they have to use special techniques; sociologists also learned that in dealing with small groups they had to develop new methods of study; and historians have handled documents differently when they are in meagre supply. The medievalist will write pages of exegesis on a single phrase and then turn with equally lengthy attention to another phrase in the same document, whereas the historian of modern times (say from the seventeenth century on), although he may sometimes give considerable attention to a single phrase, more typically goes through masses of documents, summarizing, condensing, selecting and discarding. They do not operate totally differently; the medievalist also summarizes and discards sometimes, but there is a difference in emphasis: where the supply is meagre, the document is more intensively worked over, brought into relation with a greater variety of other bits of evidence, viewed in a larger number of contexts, and when the supply is of a staggeringly great size, the prime problem is organization of the mass rather than minute attention.

For Africa before the nineteenth century (and often even during it) save in North Africa and at the Cape in the south since the seventeenth century, written documents, when we have them, are more comparable to medieval Europe in quantity than to modern Europe. We have accounts of explorers, of traders, of missionaries, of administrators, of soldiers, and of literate Africans. There are reports, letters, books, ledgers, and commercial and official records. For early periods of contact we are not likely to have many instances of a given category and not every category will be represented. As we approach the present, the written sources become fuller in number and variety. W. W. Claridge felt he could not go back beyond the nineteenth century in his *History of Gold Coast and Ashanti*[4] because the documents were insufficient. Perhaps, also, he wasn't interested, but he put himself on record that earlier historical treatment of the area was impossible. Today we have studies by Margaret Priestley on Ashanti-British relations in the eighteenth century, and by Ivor Wilks on Akwamu and on Ashanti in the seventeenth and eighteenth centuries. Both have drawn on documents that though meagre were not inadequate for the task.

Hallowell in discussing the use of similar documents for the study of American Indians in the period of early European contact, wrote:

These early observers were forced to deal with the Indians much more as differentiated personalities. Part of their task was to obtain insight into the character of the Indians in order to devise ways and means for influencing them toward certain ends. It is not surprising, then, that the missionary, the trader and the explorer reflected upon what we would call the psychological characteristics of the Indians. Consequently, we find statements here and there that refer to the character of particular individuals or to whole tribal groups.[5]

He might have added too that they were interested, for their own safety, and the traders for their trade, in the political conditions and attempted to analyse these and assess the stability of the peace or the duration and outcome of the wars.

Each of the observers inevitably had, to a greater or lesser extent, a bias, but this could be allowed for by reference to the category of the observer and by contrasting the observations of one category with another. Hallowell quotes Kinietz on this point:

In considering all of their characterizations of the Indians, it should be borne in mind that most of the Europeans wanted something: the missionaries sought converts, the traders were after furs, and the military men wanted warriors. To those who got what they desired, the Indians were sensible, brave and upright people; but if the overtures of the Europeans were not favorably received, the tribe was composed of thieves, liars, dissemblers, and even traitors.[6]

Three ways are suggested by Hallowell to contain these distortions:

The margin of error involved can be controlled, however, in several ways: (1) In most cases we have the observations of more than one person, in which case we may have corroborative testimony by independent witnesses at our disposal; (2) we can ask ourselves whether the observations make . . . sense when put side by side with other remarks and with any concrete behaviorial data cited; (3) we can evaluate the older observations in terms of our knowledge of contemporary peoples who are culturally the most conservative.[7]

The first of these controls, the weighing of different documents, needs no comment since it is the most elementary of the procedures of the critical historian. The second requires a little more caution because although this test may eliminate some assertions, it cannot prove any of them. Collingwood referred to this in his discussion of Bradley as

a criterion not of what did happen but of what could happen. It is in fact nothing but Aristotle's criterion of what is admissible in poetry; and hence it does not serve to discriminate history from fiction. It would no doubt be satisfied by the statements of an historian, but it would be satisfied no less adequately by those of an historical novelist. It cannot therefore be the criterion of critical history.[8]

The third control suggests the use of an unwritten source, ethnography, and we ought to notice here that the designation of some groups as more conservative than other groups of the same people has its dangers. What Hallowell means is that a certain group has been less in contact with Europeans and has borrowed fewer cultural traits from them, but it is never true that they have not on their own made some innovations since the time of the documented observation. Nor does the absence of borrowing mean that the 'conservative' group, minus its more recent innovations, would be equivalent to the ancestral group at the time of the earlier observation, for it is likely that the culture has been attenuated by the suppression of warfare, the interruption of old trade patterns, the elimination or degradation of natural leaders, and other factors. But these are cautions rather than denials of the usefulness of ethnographic comparisons.

A good deal more of this kind of study is possible in Africa and is needed if some of the gaps in our knowledge are to be filled, but 'ethno-history' is not the only possible use of ethnology.

Culture history, despite the shortcomings of earlier attempts, is not to be considered a repudiated concept. In America, where the 'functionalist attack on history' was not as completely successful as in Britain, culture history of the Amerindians continued to be a respected pursuit; but the more far-fetched hypotheses were not likely to survive the stringent criticism of Franz Boas and his students.

It is often thought that Franz Boas was anti-historical because he was so unmerciful in his criticisms of historical formulations, but he was concerned above all else to see that shoddy workmanship was not allowed to pass as sound scholarship. It will be of some interest therefore to note what Boas considered permissible in ethnology.

In the domain of ethnology, where for most parts of the world, no historical facts are available except those that may be revealed by archeological study, all evidence of change can be inferred only by indirect methods. . . . The method is based on the comparison of static phenomena combined with the study of their distribution. . . It is, of course, true that we can never hope to obtain incontrovertible data relating to a chronological sequence of events, but certain general broad outlines can be ascertained with a high degree of probability, even of certainty.[9]

Boas held that independent invention of simple culture traits should be presumed until other evidence of connexion could be obtained. Therefore he asserted:

the investigator must always demand continuity of distribution as one of the essential conditions for proving historical connection, and the assumption of lost connecting links must be applied most sparingly.[10]

We know of documented instances of peoples formerly in contact who are today far apart, and since there must also be many such cases among peoples whose history is unknown, or inadequately known, this stricture of Boas would remove from consideration a number of hypotheses which might have merit. In this Boas preferred the way of caution, as we should too, and if we work out the history of peoples and areas where we do not violate this principle, we might then with fuller knowledge be able to entertain the more wide-range hypotheses. When we begin with so much to be done, why jump impatiently at the grandiose schemes? It is better to accumulate gradually and surely the understanding of smaller units which will enable us to attack later the vaguer and sometimes nearly ineluctable relationships.

The historical problem that had the most interest personally for Boas was the relationship of North-eastern Asia and North-western America, and in his writing on this question we can see that he was willing to accept the validity of an argument for historical connexion based on the distribution of a complex cultural phenomenon—in this instance, Bear Ceremonies:

It is hardly admissible to assume that the cult of the bear has developed independently all over this country on account of the fear inspired by this animal, for form and content are too much alike. At the same time these particular ceremonials are not found in regard to other dangerous animals.[11]

A. L. Kroeber developed these ideas further; he emphasized the ecological setting and investigated the relationship of culture and ecology, which resulted in his *Cultural and Natural Areas of North America*; and he applied the 'Age-Area' concept, already used in biology, to culture. This is an attempt to derive time from space. The distribution of culture traits is plotted and the patterns studied. In general, it is assumed that the more widely spread traits are older than those with a more restricted distribution. We know certain instances in which this is not true. Sometimes a trait can travel exceedingly fast. The smoking of tobacco spread around the world in a matter of years, and the adoption of the growing of maize was almost parallel. But the first case is not only what the older economists used to call an 'indulgent' but is habit-forming, and the second is a nutritious food that yields more per acre than many competing plants. Keeping a cautious lookout then for such exceptional cases, we may assume that ordinarily the rate of diffusion is slower—but not necessarily uniform. The Age-Area hypothesis can be suggestive of the relative ages of traits in a given area. It is a rough measure to be backed up, if possible, by other means, linguistic or archaeological. The number of complexes clustered about the trait (i.e., the complexes into which the trait enters) also indicates age.

Mapping the distribution of traits and complexes in an area (which may contain several cultures) is helpful for the cultural history of the traits and of the area, but geography is not so useful in unravelling the history of a culture. The history of a trait is important, but the history of all traits would not give us the history of a single culture: a culture is an assemblage of traits, but it is more than the sum of the parts. Also, the history of a cultural tradition, due to diffusion, is different from the history of a people.

In any study of distributions, one must have first a typology of entities studied. We must be sure that each item counted does in fact belong to the selected category. This is not always easily established. Objects of similar form may have different functions and things which subserve the same function may have different forms. In either case, an historical connexion is possible but only precision in definition of the terms of comparison will prevent false conclusions.

Another essential consideration is the possibility of independent invention. If a trait has been invented twice in two different localities, obviously there is no historical connexion indicated; but if one area borrowed it from the other or via some intermediary, then we have an historical relationship to be investigated. How can we tell when we are dealing with diffusion and when we have an example of independent invention? This has long been a vexing problem to anthropologists and in some cases a decision cannot be made, but if we are dealing with a culture-complex wherein the details are numerous and more or less identical in the two cases, the probability of independent invention must be statistically low. For example, if in two areas we find a musical instrument of the type commonly called 'pan pipes' in which there is the same number of pipes, each of which is tuned to the same musical note, the chance of independent invention must be considered small. Or, to take a documented instance, we find in Mindanao and in Senegal that polygyny is permitted but a man is limited to four wives, and people pray five times a day. We realize that these customs are explicable by the spread of Islam, but if we had no knowledge of the history of Islam (and couldn't even find the related traits) we would conclude that there was likely to be some kind of an historical connexion because it is an arbitrary number that is specified for the maximum number of wives and the minimum number of daily prayers. The probability of peoples in different areas independently making a series of arbitrary decisions that are identical in both cases must be minimal. The more closely related the items in a complex, the more convincing the evidence. Thus the number, arrangement, and pitch of the pan pipes are more integrally related than the items of permitted number of wives and required daily prayers, since these two do not necessarily go together in any functional sense.

It is possible that supporting evidence may come from linguistics, that is, the name may be borrowed along with the trait. But the absence of linguistic evidence is not a denial of historical connexion.

In order to get a deep historical insight into a culture, it has become the practice to bring to bear upon it all the means of the various sub-divisions of anthropology (as organized in the United States); that is to say, of linguistics, of archaeology, and of the biological aspects of man, as well as of the techniques of analysing cultural and social structure.

The co-operative building of culture history by the research of many individuals in all of the branches of anthropology over a period of many years (and still continuing) is best exemplified no doubt by the work on Nuclear America, but all parts of the Americas have benefited to varying extents. The study of distributions, oral traditions, structural evidence, linguistics, archaeology, ethno-botany, ethno-zoology, and art all come within the province of anthropology. Although no single anthropologist would be likely to be competent in all of these aspects, it is helpful for historical studies to have all of these within the same profession. It is no more peculiar than the medical profession which has so many specializations that no doctor can understand them all. But by keeping the profession intact, rather than letting small specializations hive off, a certain common ground is maintained, the circulation of information is facilitated and the level of criticism is kept higher.

Although it is characteristic of American anthropology to maintain the wider definition of the 'Study of Man', it has no monopoly on studies which combine a number of approaches to the history of a people. A fine example of British scholarship is Sir John Myers' *Who Were the Greeks?* In this the ecology, physical anthropology, archaeology, traditions, and religion of the peoples of ancient Greece are brought together to provide a detailed and integrated exposition of the historical identity of the ancient people we call the Greeks. This could well serve as the model for the study of an African people, but, unfortunately, we do not have as yet any case in which the accumulated research data in the various fields approaches the quantity or richness that was available to Sir John on Greece. Synthesis, obviously, cannot take place until the basic research is done on the various aspects of a society.

The prominence given to religion by Sir John Myers is notable. Religion is a part of the culture of a people and Durkheim and others have shown how essential an understanding of the religion of a people is for an understanding of the total culture. In any except a secularized society, religion will be a key to the 'ethos', the system of values, and will illuminate by the development of rituals which are the central institutions of the society and even the functions of the institutions. Religious contracts of considerable complexity are often borrowed and offer good evidence of culture contacts. There is a good deal of published description of African religions, but relatively little has been done to draw historical inferences from it.

Religions tend to be conservative and symbols, rituals, ideological elements are often, even usually, maintained over very long periods of time, and perhaps in general longer than other types of culture-traits. They may be reinterpreted but even when this has occurred some clue of the former meaning can be found. This has in fact been the grand method of the study of religions in the ancient Middle East. It is important that we realize that this is possible, because Malinowski denied so vociferously the possibility of 'survivals' that reading the anthropological literature of the period would discourage one in considering this approach. However, Malinowski, striving to establish 'functionalism' in the hostile atmosphere of the time, went too far, as has often happened in such a case, and his brilliance carried him beyond his evidence; the result is that today we realize that no society is as completely adjusted functionally as we had been led to believe. R. K. Merton has put Malinowski's arguments in a more balanced sociological framework,[12] but as yet no modern writer has attempted to refurbish the maligned 'survival'.

Survivals that historians can use certainly exist even if their continued existence is dependent upon a new function. In an example given by Malinowski, bows and arrows are used as a children's game, they are not a survival of the past when men were hunters, he says, they have a play function. But we do not wish to deny the new function, merely to find the old, and that does not seem impossible, especially when hunting peoples using bows and arrows can still be found employing these not as toys but as weapons.

The functionalist doctrine which has given to British social anthropology its characteristic emphasis on social structure has resulted in a limitation of the field of research and has had a consequent development of the selected area of concentration. British anthropologists typically are better than their American counterparts when it comes to describing the social structure, largely because for a generation they have cultivated this subject (and a very few others) while Americans continued to spread their efforts over the whole gamut of culture *and* society, diachronically as well as synchronically.

Africa has benefited from the perfection of the social anthropologists' skills and techniques and there are some excellent monographs on the social structure of certain societies on this continent. However, this is all in the 'ethnographic present', that is, they are synchronic studies that refer only to the point in time when the study was made.

It is possible to use these synchronic studies in certain ways for historical research if we are fortunate enough to have a few favourable circumstances. For example, if we have a description of the society by an early explorer, we can compare the two descriptions for agreements and discrepancies and from this juxtaposition get suggestions of the direction of social change during the interim. If either of the accounts, or other data, indicates the probable reason or reasons for a particular kind of change, and if the inducing factor appears to have been present before the time of the earlier account, we could, as a hypothesis, project the trend of change backward beyond the time of the explorer. Of course, no trend continues forever and must at some time level out, so that we would have to be judicious in deciding how far in time it would be wise to make such an interpolation.

Oral traditions of the people, perhaps not collected by investigators of the social structure but available elsewhere in print (or waiting to be collected) can also use the synchronic study as a point of departure for an exploration backward.

I would like to say that archaeology could also be used in comparison with the structural studies of social anthropologists, but unfortunately, social anthropologists generally ignore completely in their writings the material culture of the peoples they work among, and so the archaeologist has nothing with which to compare his unearthed artifacts. In fact, at the Vienna meeting of the Congrès Internationel des Sciences Ethnologiques et Anthropologiques, the British School of Social Anthropology was criticized for having neglected to describe material culture, with the result that an archaeologist could not go to a social anthropologist's books and articles to find out such things as what tools the people used or what house types might be found. Since the archaeologist looks for continuities and wants to know if a possibility exists of a relationship between an existing culture and the site he is excavating, he habitually examines the monographs on living peoples within a wide area but has been disappointed in the reports of the social anthropologist. German studies, it might be noted to give the context of the criticism, are highly detailed and virtually exhaustive in the description of material culture. It must be admitted too that American studies, which seldom reached the standards of German work in this respect, have deteriorated in recent years and an interest in material culture is considered 'old fashioned'. It is to be hoped that the Vienna criticism will be taken to heart, in America and elsewhere as well as in Britain, so that the relationship of existing cultures and extinct ones (or of abandoned sites of existing cultures) can be more readily established. The category of material culture in an ethnographic monograph is the counterpart of the artifacts in an excavation. We must have both for comparisons and the possibilities of establishing historical relationships.

A related point is that distribution studies of items of material culture have virtually ceased to appear except from the University of Uppsala. These have a usefulness in historical studies, even if they can no longer be used in a mechanical fashion to construct 'culture circles'; but simply because their usefulness is a more modest one is no reason for despising them as, I am afraid, is the fashion.

It is possible to have a history of social structures, but this has generally been limited to societies that produced written records over a period of time. George Peter Murdock, in his *Social Structure*, suggested a method, applicable in certain circumstances, for inferring previous stages of a known social structure; but the instance in which he has used this himself— the Tuareg in his *Africa, Its Peoples and their Culture History*—has not been very convincing. I have been told that others have used this method, but I am not familiar with the results. If this method proves fruitful, it could be a boon to historical studies, but it seems to me that it still needs proving.

Evans-Pritchard[13] has pointed out that when he was a young field-worker, it took all of the time he had in the field to determine what the social structure of the group actually was and there was no time to do anything else; but the techniques of investigation have been refined so that the field worker today can determine the structure in about a quarter of the time and so has time and should investigate other things. He has also written,[14] after reading the accounts of earlier visitors to the Azande, that one cannot fully understand the contemporary culture without a knowledge of its history (so far as recoverable). This seems to be a departure from (if not a reversal of) his opinion expressed in his *Social Anthropology*, a decade earlier: that ethnology (by which he meant historical studies) and social anthropology (structural studies) were quite distinct. And if I am not mistaken, there was a disdainful attitude towards ethnology implied.

Professor Evans-Pritchard has become the outstanding proponent among British social anthropologists of historical studies, and has stated his arguments in the Marrett Lecture and in a number of articles.

A few other social anthropologists, like R. E. Bradbury as a member of the team working on the 'Benin Scheme', have been giving a good deal of time to historical aspects of African societies.

It is to be hoped that the various national schools can achieve a *rapprochement* that preserves the strong points of each. British social anthropology has pioneered and had success in the study of social structure and has thereby enriched the field for other students as well. The Americans have preserved the holistic approach and learned to see inter-relationships of different aspects of society, and they, and particularly the Germans, have maintained an interest in history. Synchronic and diachronic studies would both be furthered by closer international understanding of practitioners of the various branches of ethnological and anthropological study. But a lot of work remains to be done before we can claim to have an acceptable and accepted methodology for historical studies.

'The time has come,' the walrus said,
  'To speak of many things;
Of shoes, and ships, and sealing wax,
  And cabbages and kings.'

Lewis Carroll

CHAPTER SIX

CROPS, HERDS AND PEOPLE

THE juxtaposition of the lowly vegetable and the mighty kings was intended by Lewis Carroll to be ironic, and so it has been taken, but more recent attitudes rob it of some of its irony. No one would deny that kings were the stuff of history, but cabbages were of concern only to peasants who were not important to history (or so it used to be thought; social history has modified that point of view). We now realize that food plants can tell us a good deal of the past of the peoples who use them.

Food is obviously a very important matter for mankind from any point of view. It is claimed that we are what we eat, and therefore those who have the same diet should be the same, which is the idea behind the remark of Dr. Johnston and the rejoinder he received when he observed derisively that oats in England was food for horses but in Scotland was food for men. A Scotsman asked him, 'But where can you find such horses or such men?'

More pertinently, the way we win our food from nature is reflected in our technology, and archaeologists can tell a great deal about a society from the type and frequency of fishing gear, harvesting tools and hunting weapons that remain in the refuse of a site.

Historians have generally paid too little attention to the importance of food and food production. They have looked into the shift from a two-field system to a three-field system in medieval Europe and the introduction of the potato and the turnip to European farms. Spices are mentioned as an objective in the

search for water trade routes to South-eastern Asia, but they are only given passing mention. The importance of sugar for a certain period of history is rarely sufficiently emphasized.

Sugar is now so plentiful that it is difficult to imagine the importance it once had. Sicily, Southern Morocco, the Cape Verde Islands, the Caribbean islands, and the Philippines at various periods became important as wealth-producing sugar lands after the Westerners acquired the plant from India. The extensiveness of new lands brought into production, and eventually the cultivation of the sugar beet in cooler lands changed sugar's position from a scarcity to a surplus. But during the period of demand each area that acquired and could grow the cane had in its turn growth and decline.

ETHNO-BOTANY

But these instances are the history *of* plants and that is not the same as history *from* plants. The latter possibility is available through ethno-botany. Ethno-botany is the study of the uses of plants by various people and like anthropology, of which it is a part, it has historical applications but is not solely historically oriented. Some studies, such as Barton's on the Ifugao, survey the agricultural production and economics of a selected people, or some focus, as in South America, on the plant poisons used by indigenous peoples.

The basic principle in historical studies of this nature was stated at least as long ago as 1869 when Robert Brown wrote: 'Each genus seems to have arisen in that center in which the greatest number of its species is found; . . .'[1] In other words, differentiation requires time so that the area of greatest differentiation is the area of greatest age for that type of plant. As stated by Brown, in general terms, this applies to wild plants; but the corollary is that the oldest area of cultivation will have the greatest number of varieties of the plant, or more technically, the centre of origin will have the greatest number of cultivars of the cultigen.

To find the region, then, where a plant, perhaps now of world-wide cultivation, was originally domesticated, we look for places of great variation of cultivars. There is another check on the identification of the centre of origin in that the plant could not have been domesticated except in a place where it grew naturally, and so we look for regions which have wild relatives of the cultigen. With these two checks, both indices of differentiation, one of wild forms and one of domestic forms, we should be able to determine the geographical origin of domesticated plants, and its present distribution would then present us with the problem of the routes, stages, periods and ethnic associations of its diffusion. Geography and ecology can suggest the limitations and likelihoods of possible routes of diffusion; paleobotany may furnish confirmation by fossil plants and perhaps suggest a chronology for the site of the fossil; present ethnic association with the plants, linguistics and oral traditions may help to indicate the peoples responsible for the spread of the crop.

As presented above, the method seems very precise and it is in fact one of the promising means to historical reconstruction, but there are problems in this method and it is not quite as simple as it seems at first glance. Sometimes botanists are not able to find wild relatives and sometimes it is extremely difficult to distinguish wild relatives from feral offshoots or weed forms that have arisen from the cultigen.

Until recently, the case of the sweet potato was the outstanding example of an historical ethno-botanical study. This pointed to a connexion between South America and the western Pacific islands. The banana, cotton and other plants raise questions about relationships between Africa and Asia.

George Peter Murdock in his *Africa: Its Peoples and Their Culture History* has extensively discussed the botanical factor in African history. Whether or not all of his particular formulations stand the test of criticism, he has the distinction of opening for wide discussion questions of food crops in the history of Africa and has stimulated further study of these problems.

Murdock suggests an independent African centre of domestication which he calls the Sudanic complex and locates it in the region of the upper Niger. It includes the cereals: fonio, pearl millet, and sorghum; the legumes: cow peas; the tubers: coleus, Bambara groundnut, geocarpa and Guinea yam; the leaf vegetable: okra; the vines: tamerind and akee; the condiments: kola and red sorrel; the fibres: cotton and ambary; and the oil plants: oil palm, sesame, and shea.

This is postulated to be uninfluenced by other centres and approximated as 5,000 years old. Some objections to this formulation are that it ignores the distribution of neolithic artifacts in the Sahara and North Africa[2] which indicate that, in a wetter phase, the Sahara connected the Sudan to the North African and Middle Eastern agricultural regions in an unbroken continuum; and the plants inventory of this complex argues diversity of origin in that some, such as kola and oil palm are forest plants while the others are savannah plants. Also the story of cotton is far more complex than Murdock indicates. Some of these plants are sown; some vegetatively propagated; quite different techniques.

Vavilov had earlier proposed an Abyssinian centre of origin and Murdock accepts and incorporates this into his scheme. Vavilov found 19 crops, including 4 hard wheats, 5 oil plants, 6 spices, 4 vegetables and 4 miscellaneous.[3]

Both of these presentations represent Africa as participating in the process of domesticating food plants rather than being the passive recipient of the crops and techniques of cultivation from elsewhere. Many of the plants that are important to the diet of various African peoples are alien in origin. The banana and some yams are from South-east Asia and maize and manioc were introduced from America. Most scholars, other than R. Porteres, and Vavilov, the botanists, and Murdock and F. R. Irvine, who studied the indigenous foods crops, had emphasized the exotic plants and virtually ignored the indigenous crops. Particularly prolific are the writings of the 'Indonesian' school, if one may call them that, who see the essential foods and many cultural features as well coming into Africa originally from South-eastern Asia.

Many of the latter group postulate a kind of void before the arrival of the traits that they have traced. It is not necessary to assume that Africans were hunters before obtaining Asian crops any more than it is necessary to assert that Italians, who eat a great deal of *pasta* and tomato sauces, must have been hungry before Marco Polo brought spaghetti back from China and the tomato was introduced from the New World.

The obvious fact is that one kind of plant food often replaces another. Habituation to one kind of plant may pre-dispose a people to the borrowing of one rather than another exotic

plant when there is such a choice. It has been suggested that in
West Africa, Asiatic rice was adopted in areas where an indigenous oryza was cultivated, whereas cassava tended to be
adopted in yam areas,[4] but some localities do not fit this
generalization and we would have to say that ecology as well
as tradition affects borrowing[5] of new food crops.

How much do we actually know about the origins and spread
of agriculture? Many theories have been put forward to explain
the discovery or invention of agriculture.

Eduard Hahn[6] observed that in the hunting-gathering
societies there was a division of labour on sexual lines: the men
specializing in hunting and the women in gathering roots,
berries, seeds, and edible insects. Men therefore would learn
the psychology of the herd animals and, where they were
plentiful, follow them and chase away other predators for which
the animals would be thankful; a symbiotic relationship set
up in this way led to domestication. Women, on the other hand,
found out the most productive locality of vegetable foods and
groups of women collectors laid claim to certain territories for
collection. Perhaps from spilling seed they discovered from the
subsequent prolific yield at that spot that it was possible to sow
seed annually and increase the yield. Thus in groups where the
food supply came predominantly from animals there evolved a
pastoral form of society, but on the other hand, where the food
supply was more abundantly provided by the gathering activities of the women, tilling cultures emerged. Men, then, invented pastoralism and women invented hoe cultures. This
seemed to fit the observation that matrilineal societies were
usually tillers but that pastoralists had a predilection for
patrilineality. Hahn's idea was adopted by Franz Oppenheim
who saw the origin of the state in the conquest of tillers by
pastoralists.

But this early theory does not satisfy the later observation
that pastoralists are never quite independent of plant foods.
They either trade with tillers or raid them; or they have sub-
sidiary crops of their own, perhaps reluctantly, as Evans-
Pritchard showed to be the case with Nuer. Owen Lattimore
gave reasons for believing that the nomadic pastoralists of *The
Inner Asian Frontiers of China* had been derived for a society with
mixed agriculture, i.e. one with both domesticated plants *and*

animals. The earliest archaeological records of the Middle Eastern and Egyptian civilizations show them to have had such a mixed agriculture. A. L. Kroeber called pastoralists a 'half-society' in that they were partially dependent upon a relationship with tillers.

V. G. Childe suggested that desiccation in the Libyan desert and the Middle East might have driven men and animals into the oases and river valleys, that men took over the organization of the water holes, and that animals and plants were domesticated simultaneously.

C. Sauer[7] argues that plants were domesticated by fishermen for their fibre and some were found to have food value also; and that when plant food was available, the planters used some of it to feed selected young animals, retrieved when their mothers were killed by hunters of the group, and in this way domesticated animals. For Sauer, the domestication of plants was the prerequisite for the domestication of animals, but others have urged the opposite: that cereals (allegedly the first domesticates) were cultivated to feed the already domesticated cattle, but this is definitely a minority opinion.

Thus some writers have suggested that plants and animals were domesticated independently, while others suggested that one was dependent on the other; and some think this occurred simultaneously, whereas others think it was seriatim; and there are differences of opinion as to the order. Obviously, there can be little certainty yet, but the problem is not insoluble.

Sauer's thesis, which is a very ingenious yet plausible one, also involved a localization in South-east Asia with an emphasis upon plants that are propagated by suckers or tubers. The transplanting of these, he refers to as the Planting Culture, and it was only later, he claims, with diffusion of food growing beyond the Monsoon area that sowing of seed was learned as a substitute for 'planting'.

Western Asia, the cradle of civilization, where the 'urban revolution' first took place, according to this thesis got its agriculture from Malaysia but via India and in a modified form. This argument is at variance with the usual interpretation that has the diffusion go in the opposite direction. But some do not postulate a connexion between the two. Kroeber inclines to the possiblity of an independent invention of agriculture in the two areas and another in Middle America.

One might claim that the dense population of eastern and southern Asia indicates a long existence of agriculture in the region; but it can be countered that rice, as a particularly productive grain, permitted a faster growth of population than some other plants. And against Sauer's notion is the archaeological record which shows South-eastern Asia as late and secondary in its development in the Stone Ages; this, of course, does not eliminate the possibility but lessens the probability that cultivation of plants originated in that region.

The significance of this for African history is that, if Sauer is correct, Africa was a late and passive recipient of agriculture. At the moment, however, it does not appear that the earliest concern with cultivated plant food was derived from Malaysia, but F. Simoons has raised the possibility that the ensete of Ethiopia is a relic of an old 'planting culture'. At any rate, it cannot be denied that in a later phase the continent did receive some important crops from that quarter.

Another approach, and one based on the most detailed botanical research thus far, has been suggested by E. Anderson. He has been more concerned with the process of domestication than with the region in which it took place. Cultigens are different from other plants; they are hardier and can grow in a greater variety of edapic conditions. They share this characteristic with weeds, to some of which many of the cultigens are closely related. Domestication resulted from the settlements of man, creating 'scars' in the natural vegetation cover in which weeds could spring up, and the rubbish heaps of the camp would contain pips of wild fruits and refuse of other collected plant food. Some introduced seeds would flourish. Mutations would have a better chance of survival; and hybrids that could not occur in nature because of difference of habitat would appear. The useful new varieties would be preserved and further selected by man. In this way, he believes, domestication came about gradually and at first beyond the consciousness of man. But eventually man deliberately took plants with him when he moved and this resulted in the juxtaposing of semi-domesticated plants with wild plants of related but distinct species. New hybrids appeared with new traits from which the useful ones

were preserved and developed by selection and cultivation, and
the useless ones survive as weeds.

'It is quite likely,' he writes, 'that a good many of our crops
were not originally used for purposes we would now suppose the
only reason for growing them.' Cotton, for example, may have
been at first utilized as an oil-seed and the lint appeared *after*
cultivation. In regard to Murdock's formulation, we might note
that this plant may have been first used in Africa—but probably first produced useful lint in India.

In fact, Anderson noted in passing that several other plants
also suggest an old connexion between Africa and India.

Suppose that very early in the origin of agriculture, say in the
Neolithic or earlier, an agricultural people had colonized India
from Africa, taking with them the seeds to start one of their crude,
weedy garden-rubbish-heap-orchards. When they reached India
some of their crops would be in an area where wild relatives were
growing, different from any of those they had previously been
mingling with. The resulting hybrids would have given a special
variability to this area . . .[8]

Although this suggestion is not further developed, it seems to
imply that perhaps the very earliest agricultural beginnings
were in some unspecified part of Africa. The stages necessary
for the development of cultigens would account for the greater
richness of Asia in number and variety of crops, and the relative poverty of Africa in this respect does not eliminate it from
consideration as the (or a) centre of origin as generally believed.

This suggestion fits in with the paleolithic and the palaeonto-
logical records in that it now appears plausible—and in fact
most likely—that mankind evolved on the African continent, for
only here has an 'osteodontokeratic' phase in the development
of technology been found. This is Raymond Dart's term for the
still somewhat controversial pre-Stone-Age culture type that
utilized bone and antler tools. And in Africa 'pebble-tools', the
oldest type of Stone-Age tool, are found in sequences that lead
uninterruptedly to the end of the paleolithic. Africa was, in the
Old Stone Age, an area of origination and innovation, the
'culture-focus', the leader in the lithic civilization. In the
Neolithic it lost the initiative to the Fertile Crescent, but it is
creditable that the incipient phase of plant growing took place

here—especially since the oldest pottery, thought of as a neo-lithic trait, yet found was discovered in Africa.

Conflicting theories in the field will continue for some time, no doubt, to plague us in our efforts to understand Africa's ethno-botanical history; for such grandiose theories as that of Sauer are not easy to prove or disprove. But on some levels there need not be conflict. Those who assume more than one centre of domestication can accept Sauer's South-east Asian complex without his insistence on its priority in time or its origination of the other complexes. That the search for fibres was important in the discovery of food plants and that fishermen were inclined towards this search is accepted by Anderson, but for him it is not the only non-nutritive motive. Magic may also have played a part, as early man seemed to have adopted certain plants as efficacious in warding off spirits. They would all, for whatever reason collected, act in a similar fashion in the camp's 'rubbish-heap'.

The study of weeds can also give us historical leads. About four-fifths of the weeds in the United States are not native but came from Europe with the crops they accompany. Where do Africa's weeds come from? And where are African weeds to be found? Are there any in India (as we might expect from Anderson's suggestion mentioned above)? In the tropics we are handicapped because there are many so-called pan-tropical weeds which, being found in the tropics in every continent, tell us nothing. But perhaps they raise a problem by their existence. How did they originate—as *weeds*—and become dispersed so widely? Many American weeds are found in African forests, no doubt some came with maize, manioc, etc., but others have come in more recently. The Sudan has many indigenous weeds, arguing the antiquity of its agriculture, but the inventory of weeds has not been fully catalogued as to origin. The importance of this was put by Anderson: 'The history of weeds is the history of man'.

ETHNO-ZOOLOGY

Animals used by man can be studied in the same way, and ethno-zoology, which as Murdock points out is more difficult to handle, can also yield us historical inferences.

Are there any animals that were domesticated in Africa? It is not infrequently said that there are not. But the ass and the cat are now generally accepted as having been brought into man's society in North-eastern Africa. The dog is often thought of as having been the first animal domesticated because it is the most widely spread and some peoples who have neither other animals nor domesticated plants have the dog. It has been rather too facilely conjectured that the dog helped palaeolithic man in his hunting. But archaeology has failed to find dog bones in any site older than the mesolithic. Sauer says there are wild dogs in South-east Asia and therefore it must have been there that it was tamed. But it is not clear whether these are originally wild or merely feral—i.e. escapés from domestication. Central Africa also has wild dogs but I do not claim to know whether they are feral or not. However, they are homogeneous in shape and size, which argues against former domestication. Cattle are claimed for Western Asia, but wild cattle ranged northern Africa from Morocco to Egypt. It has been suggested by a French writer that they were domesticated in the Sahara before it became desiccated and we know there were cattle-keeping people there because they have left rock paintings of themselves and their cattle; but others of his countrymen have criticized his reasoning. Hathor, the cow-goddess of Egypt, it is suggested by Levy in *The Gate of Horn*, may have been introduced by people from the Western Desert who had a similar goddess.

It may be that some breeds were domesticated in Asia and some in Northern Africa. A close attention to type is necessary. There is a small Maghrebine cattle which is perhaps related to the West African 'dwarf cattle'. Either or both might be descendants of a wild African progenitor. The study of Joshi and Phillips for F.A.O. on the description and distribution of breeds of African cattle should be useful in unravelling the routes of diffusion of different types of cattle.

The Zebu is apparently an Asiatic, and perhaps specifically Indian, type. It is now widely spread in Africa and all writers, with whom I am familiar, who have discussed its introduction have assumed a land migration of pastoralists bringing this type of humped cattle with them. However, there are drawings of Phoenicians in an eighteenth-dynasty mural unloading humped cattle from a ship. If the Phoenicians brought them to Egypt (whence?), they may also have introduced them to African coastal peoples further south, and no population movement need be postulated to account for its transfer.

The horse is certainly an animal of extra-African origin. There were small horses in Palaeolithic Europe, and larger ones were brought in from Asia. In Africa, there are three types according to Doutressoulle: one perhaps being related to the small European horse, another the 'Barb', a type of old North African formation, and the Arabian horse. The distribution of these in the Sudan presents some interesting possibilities of relationship to other culture traits, a subject on which I hope to write more fully in the near future. Professor Kohler of Köln University has studied the words for horse in certain languages to try to discover the likely direction of linguistic (and therefore zoologic) borrowing. More of this type of research is needed on other African languages where the horse is used. The distribution of equestrian wood-carvings, and their styles, might be enlightening on the spread of the horse itself. Oral traditions and proverbs about horses also need investigation.

Goats and sheep are the most widely distributed domestic animals in Africa. These animals are good candidates for being the first domesticates, and although this probably happened in western Asia they must have been introduced into Africa very early because they have not gone through some of the changes subsequent to domestication that are found elsewhere. Some African sheep, for example, and apparently most of them, do not produce wool. Are those that do, post-European imports? The black and white markings show an interesting regional distribution that might repay study.

The pig, although known in ancient Egypt, was only introduced in the south in European times. Murdock wondered about this[9] but the answer is in the linguistics, as their names for the animal, I am told by Professor J. B. Greenberg, are derived from Portuguese. There are a few pictures of pigs in the Saharan rock-paintings.

The bee seems to have more prominence in eastern Africa than elsewhere except the Senegambia, and the related traits of the particular uses of honey and honey-wine (or mead) should help to indicate the paths of its spread. In fact, methods of food preparation of any kind of food and food taboos are cultural traits that should be studied in conjunction with the above biological specimens. Techniques of stone-boiling, oven-building, fermenting, pounding in mortars, milking, drinking warm blood, drying, smoking, salting and storing are useful in plotting the diffusion of the food sources. The use of animals in transport is also of interest, although it seems only to be found among the Hottentots and in the Sudan, and North and North-eastern Africa.

Finally, we might note that man is himself a domestic animal,[10] domesticated by culture and sharing the same kinds of variation exhibited by other domesticated animals; and that in Darwin's opinion, Mankind originates in Africa, since two of his three closest relatives are native there. The Chimpanzee and Gorilla are only found in Africa; the Orang-utang is only found in the southern Asian islands.

HUMAN BIOLOGY

Ethno-zoology can in a sense then be seen as cognate to human biology or physical anthropology. Hopes have often been expressed for the use of anthropometry in historical research. Franz Boas assures us:

The statistical study of types will lead to an understanding of the blood-relationship between types. It will consequently be a means of reconstructing the history of the mixture of human types. It is probable that it will also lead to the establishment of a number of good types which have remained permanent through long periods.[11]

The use of the word types is intended to convey that not only mixtures between races but mixtures between sub-races within a single race could be studied in this way.

This hope has never been realized in substantial measure, but the method itself has not been invalidated. Cautions have been pointed out by various anthropologists, usually in commenting on the hypotheses put forward on inadequate data, and opinions vary on the importance of this type of evidence for historical reconstruction. However, as yet no study based on sufficiently broad samples, scientifically selected and carefully measured, has been made. Perhaps this is partly because the number of people within a group and the number of groups that must be measured for this type of historical study is far greater than that necessary for a simple description of general types. Here again, as in so many other branches of anthropological study, the specialists have only been occasionally interested in the historical aspects of their subject. Historians trying to draw inferences from the meagre data, collected with other ends in view, are therefore handicapped by the paucity of anthropometric measurements available, and they have sometimes been unfamiliar with the requirements for a rigidly scientific handling of the material that was in hand.

There are many suggestions in the literature that tall chiefs in certain areas are indications of former 'Nilotic' or 'Hamitic' conquest, but these statements, as already indicated, are highly impressionistic. Small chiefs are ignored and no averages are ever obtained, and, most suspiciously, these claims smack of C. G. Seligman's hypothesis that all the history of Africa is a series of 'Hamitic' invasions of Negro areas. Although his book, *The Races of Africa* was recently reprinted, it is no more accurate now than when it first appeared, and there is now less excuse for putting forward this inept formulation.[12]

Until there has been a good deal more, and better, anthropometric study of the peoples of Africa, little can be done that will be of historical significance. The studies that exist are invariably on small samples, sometimes improperly assembled, and the scatter of the studies over the great extent of the continent makes comparison fraught with difficulty.

There are other problems which a mere accumulation of series of population measurements will not, of itself, overcome. Before we talk about mixtures of types we must have precise definitions of the types.

Actually the type of a population is always an abstraction of the striking peculiarities of the mass of individuals . . . What the striking peculiarities are depends largely upon the previous experiences of the observer, not upon the morphological value of the observed traits. This explains the diversities of opinion in taxonomic classification. They all contain so many subjective elements without necessary morphological checks that conclusions based upon them have slight value. A result of historical significance can be obtained only by a study of the many genetic lines contributing the population, not selected from the arbitrary point of view of which is 'typical', but with due consideration of the variety of forms that occur, of their frequencies in succeeding generations, and of their response to varying environmental influences.[13]

Thus to collect a truly random sample for measurement is not enough; we must have more than individuals *qua* individual: we must also have studies of mature individuals within families; and we must know something of the 'plasticity' of the type, i.e. within what limits it can vary and what factors engender such variation—this latter is something about which we are not yet well informed. The following criticism by Boas of generalizations made about European populations (where the anthropometric data that has been collected is far more ample than in Africa) illustrates the dangers implicit in this kind of material.

We might claim that the frequency of various values of head-index in southern Italy indicates descent from distinct hereditary groups and that a certain percentage of 'Alpin' types have intermingled with the 'pure' Mediterranean strain; or we might claim that the frequency of blue eyes in Sicily corresponds to the amount of Norman blood. These conclusions are valueless if it cannot be shown that the cephalic index is solely determined by heredity and that in a 'pure' race its variations do not exceed very narrow limits, and that blue eyes may not originate by mutation, as they certainly must have done at one time, and that this mutation may not occur again in any one of the strongly de-pigmented European populations.[14]

Franz Weidenreich has since put forward a very convincing case that the cephalic index is subject to evolutionary pressures and that dolichocephalism (long-headedness) tends to give way and eventuate in brachycephalism (round-headedness).[15] This might seem to remove all possibility of using the cephalic index (or perhaps any somatic or skeletal index) to unravel the history of population mixtures, but Weidenreich is dealing with the entire evolutionary series of human and hominid remains and it seems permissible to attempt to analyse a particular case within a limited time period if the data was collected according to the proper research design and in sufficient quantity. Perhaps we should also keep in mind that Boas is considering the question of proof and is accordingly very stringent (as is appropriate in such a case), but we can always use inferences which

we cannot immediately prove (or which may not be susceptible to proof) but which in conjunction with other types of
evidence can have a definite value.

Another branch of human biology, serology, which uses a
different type of data, claimed by some to be more genetically
representative, can be used to supplement the anatomical
measurements. The earliest analysis of blood distinguished the
ABO types, but now MN, Rh and many 'abnormal' haemoglobins are also known. Each individual tested will be shown to
have either A, or B, or AB, or O type, also to have either M or
N, to be Rh positive or negative, to show the presence or
absence of the various 'abnormal' haemoglobins. Different individuals in the same population will have different types, but the
population can be characterized by the percentages of the
possible types. The different factors may vary independently,
it seems, but so far most of the data available is on the ABO
series. Thus we can make distinctions of neighbouring peoples
who have sharply different blood group pictures and establish
that they do not, or at least did not until recently, form a
single gene pool (a group within which matings can occur);
and we can compare more distantly separated peoples who have
similar blood group pictures and consider the possibility of
relationships. As we might expect, however, suppositions of
relationship have to be handled with caution. William C. Boyd
tells us:

The ABO data alone do not enable us to separate the peoples of the
world into clear-cut races which make much sense geographically:
they would for example force us to put some of the American Indians,
the Australian aborigines, and the Baffin Land Eskimos into the
same race, which hardly makes sense.[16]

But the A antigen can be divided into two sorts of A, A_1
and A_2 which can give us a further precision, and if other blood
types are added, uncertainties can be proved or eliminated.
As A. C. Allison puts it:

If we were to rely upon ABO frequencies alone, we might be
tempted to equate the people of England with Arabs from Yemen,
Hungarians, certain Melanesians and Micronesians, etc. . . .
whereas further blood-grouping tests—as well as other anthropological characters—resolve these populations into a number of
quite distinct stocks.[17]

The blood groups were selected for study by some geneticists because it was until recently thought that the blood types were not adaptive, that is, did not change in response to environmental factors; but now the common viewpoint is that all physical characteristics are to some extent adaptive, and this means that for any but short-range interpretations this factor must be taken into consideration. None the less, serological research is a promising field which is of considerable importance to the elucidation of population history.

Where there has been a mixture of Caucasian and Negro, a test developed by Glass and Li can show the proportions of each in the mixture if it is recent. This might for some purposes be interesting for studies of the Swahili, Cape Coloured or Creole peoples, but it would probably not be able, unfortunately, to tell us if the Haratin are an old stock or an ancient cross of Berber and Sudanese.

EPIDEMIEOLOGY

Abnormal haemoglobins, particularly S and C, show distributions that have historical significance, and, among other things, they are related to the problem of disease. Medical historical studies, hardly yet conceived for this continent, are given a good earnest by an article of Livingston in the *American Anthropologist* in which he suggested that malaria is a disease of agriculturalists because they clear the forests and allow surface water to accumulate; but that hunting groups are less affected. This seems consistent with the distribution of Haemoglobin S, and so-called sickle cell.

Yaws, leprosy and other diseases need to be investigated, and diseases of domestic animals as well. Cattle must give way before the tsetse fly. It is said that the tsetse fly is expanding at a rate of one hundred square miles a year. It should be possible, if one can postulate an even rate of this expansion, to work out from the plotted area of its present occupation, not only approximately when its expansion began, but about where the mutation occurred—or whatever it was—that started this fly on its disease-spreading career. If we could determine the distribution of this disease at various periods in the past, it would aid us in understanding the expansion of pastoralism on the continent.

The problems involved in bio-historical research are many and various, and exemplify the difficulties of historical reconstruction from unwritten sources. In practice, however, one would take only a small part of the spectrum here surveyed, and by concentration within confined limits, as, let us say, of beekeeping or the use of sorghum, be able to add to our knowledge of Man in Africa. Little by little we will be able to put together such bits until we get a larger picture. Speaking only about the botanical aspect, Anderson said, 'When with something like this precision [i.e. the knowledge that has been obtained about sunflowers] we are able to detail the development of a score or so of the worlds major crops we shall be able to write the prehistory of man.'[18]

Kunst: eine andere Nature, auch geheimnisvoll, aber verstand-
licher; denn sie entspringt aus dem Verstande.

Goethe

CHAPTER SEVEN

THE TESTIMONY OF ART

THERE are two bodies of literature on African art that until recently were quite distinct. One was frequently represented by large, profusely illustrated and expensive books; the other more often by articles in obscure journals, more likely than not illustrated only by line drawings, inadequate both in number and in their power to convey the total effect of the originals. Curiously, the readers of the first were often unaware of the existence of the second. Some still are. The first type deals with the more or less contemporary plastic art; the second with the engravings and paintings on rock surfaces, some recent, but much of it quite old—often several millennia. In Africa, these are usually not in caves but in more or less open shelters of the type the French call *abri*.

The wood carvings—masks and statuettes—are the best known of the plastic arts from Africa. It is said that Vlaminck was the first of the European artists to appreciate African art and to help start the kind of artistic cult that grew up around it. This was of course merely part of the process of the adoption of non-western art by European artists and public in this century; it came a bit later than the adoption of Japanese prints, which were a 'civilized' art, but before some of the other 'primitive' art styles.

The effect of African art on European painting and sculpture is an interesting topic, outside the strict sphere of our concern here, but it is worth observing that along with African music it was an item in the cultural borrowing by Europe from Africa. It is difficult to separate the influence of African art from that of the other non-western styles, but we might be

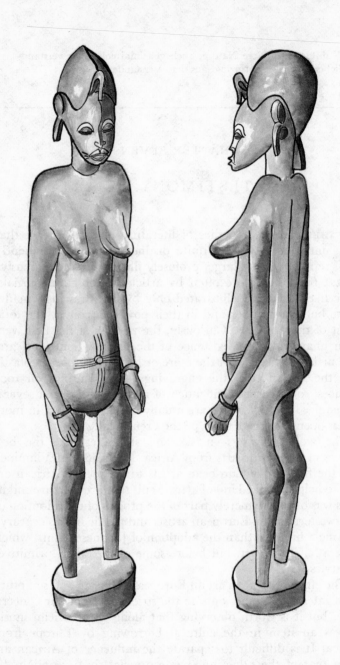

warned that the expectation of originality tends to obscure some of the borrowing: e.g. Modigliani's friend Lipschitz denies that African art affected Modigliani's painting, and yet in the stylization of nearly all of his faces one can see not just African, but specifically the Baoulé characteristics.

Returning our attention to the African aspects of our subject, we find that the writings on wood-sculpture are almost always non-historical in character (although the bronze castings are sometimes so dealt with), but the rock-art on the other hand is typically discussed in historical terms. I do not believe that this distinction is logical, but it is easy to see how it arose.

Plastic arts since they could be transported were adopted by the European collectors and appeared in museums, artists' studios, art and curio shops, and were found to lend themselves to the decor of modern homes. The items became expensive (and forgeries were not unknown) and there was a demand for the books of photographs. The rock-art, however, could not be transported to Europe and was often inaccessible and difficult to photograph; and until Henri Lhote had painters copy the 'frescoes' of the Tassili region of the Sahara, there was no extensive collection of accurate representations of this *art rupestre* that gave both the original size and colour. I have seen these copies in the basement of the Musée de l'Homme in Paris and they are truly impressive. There are others in the Frobenius Institute in Frankfort. Reproductions in bound volumes are available and perhaps rock-art will now become fashionable in the large, expensive art books and sit on the shelves alongside the Lascaux cave paintings and African plastic art.

So then it may be that both categories will be adopted by the aesthetes, but will both be adopted by the historians?

It is understandable that much of the writing on African sculpture should be from the aesthetic point of view, but judging from the writings on European art, there is an interest on the part of the same reading public for both art interpretation, stylistic analysis and art history.

The things that obstruct art history in Africa are the termites and the climate, which soon destroy wood carvings, the paucity of archaeological excavations which might yield us some old stone, ivory or bronze sculpture, and the total lack of a literary record concerning art. The Arabic writers, being Moslems, could hardly take notice of representational art; in fact, they seem not to have been interested even in geometric art. The early Europeans passed it by in silence or with very general and usually depreciatory remarks. However, are we so sure that there are no old pieces in Europe? Recently, searches in European archives for written records of Africa have begun; why do we neglect the search in private collections and museums for older pieces of African sculpture? They were always 'curios' before they became the fashion, and some Portuguese family houses, perhaps in an old storage room, or the Vatican museum or some religious order's headquarters may have some things that would help us to understand the age of particular styles and the stability of the styles.

At the moment, the style about which we know most historically is that of the Benin bronzes. This is partly because of an interest in the origin of the knowledge of casting by the *ciré perdu* method rather than an investigation of the history of the art itself, although there has been great interest in this style since it became known in Europe at the end of the nineteenth century. When the British captured Benin City at the end of the nineteenth century, Europe suddenly became aware of this style, and General Pitt-Rivers was able, virtually overnight, to expand his private museum from a collection of old guns to a far more interesting African art museum. Speculation was rife for decades afterwards as to whether it was the Portuguese, or perhaps the Carthaginians (who were never taken too seriously) who introduced bronze and the technique of casting. It was unfashionable in those days—when Lord Lugard was talking about the 'child-races' of mankind and Seligman,[1] at times, sounded like de Gobineau's apostle to Africa—to suppose that the Africans could have developed this art themselves.

Benin's oral tradition affirmed that the Beni learned it from the Ife—that is, from Africans inland rather than from whites on the coast. Archaeological finds of bronze castings there, particularly the Ife heads, make this seem very likely; and that the existence of bronze among the Beni pre-existed the Portuguese presence is now evident by the stage in the evolution of the Benin style at which the representations of Portuguese first appear.

Not much has been done, except in the Benin case, to relate

the traditions of African peoples to their art, although as William Fagg noted:

. . . some of the most important of the art-producing tribes themselves have historical traditions, orally transmitted indeed, but often convincing enough after collation of variant versions. And it is probable that far more of such unwritten history remains to be collected and evaluated. . . . At present we certainly do not have enough knowledge to attempt to reconstruct a comprehensive history—and still less an art history—of the Guinea Coast.[2]

He goes on to deplore the 'unrestricted speculation' that exists when there should be systematic collecting and interpreting of oral traditions and of course archaeological excavation. Nigeria, which has an antiquities service, is making a steady progression with archaeological research, and much of the material found is in the field of the art historian. That Benin art derived from Ife seems likely and that modern Yoruba art came from the same source seems likely. Or perhaps Ife was a specialization of the more widespread Yoruba style. Whether this in turn came from Nok is a more perplexing problem, hampered at the moment by the lack of intervening stages in the evolution, if such it was, from the far earlier Nok to the later but still pre-European Ife. It is possible, however, that Nok continued for some time after the latest C14 date that we have at the moment.[3] The two cultures, Nok and Yoruba, are more or less continuous in space.

The relation of the media to each other deserves closer attention. What happens to a wood carving style when it is applied to ivory? Would we recognize as the work of one people their stone and wood styles? Probably not. Is it easier to transmit a terracotta style to bronze than a wood technique to ivory? These are natural pairs, at any rate, corresponding to the antithesis between modelling and carving. At Benin the wood and ivory carvings were made by the same craftsmen (the *igbesanewa*) and the bronzes and terracottas were made by another group (the *iguneromivo*); in each case the styles were identical, but the first pair are different from the second. [This was pointed out to me by William Fagg.] Until we know more of the answers to questions like these it will be difficult to see the historical and stylistic relationships of the total continuum of African art.

Little has been done to achieve detailed stylistic analyses of each tribal style in order that relationships can be investigated. In European art we know that the Byzantine traditions were transmitted to Sienna and from there spread adaptively throughout Italy. Later, artists from the Low Countries went to Italy to study, so that we can establish a continuous connexion through quite variant styles from Flemish art to Byzantium.

Could we without the literary record achieve the same kind of thing in Africa? It is certainly worth trying. In the example above, note the position of Sienna in the sequence. It is critical as the gateway of Byzantine knowledge of the preparation of art materials, but the later Italian painters diverged widely from the Siennese in style. If we did not know of Sienna's position in Italian art history we might ignore the work of the artists of this unimportant city and call it aberrant or unrepresentative of Italy, but it in fact shows in its 'aberrant' features the links which are historically significant. Only by an exhaustive collection that strives to find all styles, regardless of aesthetic appeal, and then by thorough stylistic analysis of the treatment of detail and proportion in the conception of the figure and also as far as possible an analysis of technique of working the materials and of the tools employed, only then can we attempt to put forward hypotheses of the historical relationships between existing tribal styles. Even then this is likely to be possible only in a few cases, but it would be worthwhile to have these leads. In other cases the rate of change may have been too fast in the various diverging lines for the preservation of evidence of distinct affinities. Thus we are unlikely to obtain a comprehensive scheme of art history in this manner and we should be cautious of attempts to construct grandiose theories.

Even here we would be handicapped because we would not have a mass of materials in which were mixed items of various ages that could be ranged in a series so that their relative chronology would correspond to the age of Byzantium, of Sienna, of Florence and of Flanders. Those that represented Byzantium in the African analogue would be known only by recent works, and the style would have had time to further evolve, or be influenced by other styles, or change in various ways. All styles thus would have to be considered as the end product of a long line of development. How could we distinguish between a similarity that was the result of the convergence of two quite different styles, and one that was only the modification of a former identity? Perhaps sometimes we couldn't, and at any rate there could be no firm certainty in many cases. But since we would have analysed the treatment of detail—for example, the way the eye is represented, or the ear, the hair or hands—we might expect that, if there were earlier a very high degree of similarity when one group borrowed the conception (and possibly, even the tools) from another, that subsequent changes would not affect each detail at once. In other words, the way of representing the hair might change but many of the other details be unchanged. Thus we could form classes that treated certain things in the same manner. Those tribes that shared a number of classes would presumably have some historic connexion; the larger the number of features in common, the greater the probability that there had been artistic borrowing and the more recent it must have been.

To attempt this at all requires tedious attention to detail; and the kind of nonsense sometimes found in the literature on African art, which compares two styles in terms of 'a severity of abstraction', must be superseded if anything is to be accomplished.

We should not, perhaps, expect too much from this method, for the art traditions are most likely very old and there has been time for great elaboration. However, if we cannot reach back to the trunk and the roots, we could certainly identify the branches.

Exactly how old these traditions are, we may not be able to determine. Frobenius suggested that the European Palaeolithic stone figures were probably a development out of a woodcarving tradition. He reasoned that wood was easier to work than stone and ought therefore to have preceded it; the stone sculpture resulted from a woodland people from the south arriving in the treeless glacial tundras of Pleistocene Europe and transferring their wood-carving techniques to stone for lack of the familiar material. This implies that the original home of wood carving was in the south, perhaps in Africa, and that African art might be as old as (or actually older than) the Gravettian culture.

African art could possibly be that old (although it is probably not quite so hoary), but its age does not depend on the reasoning of Frobenius, with whom one can easily pick an argument. Does wood-carving of figurines necessarily precede stone sculpture among a people who make their tools from stone? If they preferred wood to stone as a medium, even the tundra could have provided a piece a few inches long, since the figures in question are small.

It would probably be best not to concentrate on ultimate origins yet, but to give attention to the more recent periods. I have often thought that the kingdoms were responsible for spreading a particular style (or features of a style) among neighbouring peoples. Let us note that Abomey was surrounded by a series of villages that furnished the capital with pottery, wood carving, bronze casting, cloth and other things. It is my opinion that this was typical. The Bakuba chief commissioned a wood-carver who would eventually commemorate him in an appropriate seated wooden figure. In one way or another, royalty was the patron of the arts. This factor is seldom emphasized. It is true that art also had religious functions; but not all art was religious art, although that generalization is frequently asserted. Nor can all art be explained in the pseudo-Freudian clap-trap of those writers who know nothing of African societies but spin everything out of their theories and their fantasies. Some art work was for the ornamentation of the palace and the pleasure of its occupants; it was a secular art. Even the religious art, in fact, might at times have political subsidies; in a strong kingdom it would be better supported than in a less highly organized society. This would be so because of the intertwining of the political and the religious systems, and this relationship, on the other hand, might also tend to eliminate the distinction I have made, for there may often be a religious component in the ornamental works.

Ancient Ghana, being pagan, was most likely a producer of art. We don't, as we have admitted, know the age of the wood-carving tradition; bronze casting cannot be confidently dated in the known instances, such as Ife or Gao, to the supposed time of Ghana's foundation in the third or fourth century A.D.; but terra-cotta heads from Nok sites are considerably older than this. But if Ghana had artists, did Mali also? Mali, it is to be remembered, was Islamic and Islam forbids representational art. It has been argued, for instance, by William Fagg, that 'It is improbable . . . that the Sudanese empires practised any but the geometric art of Islamic cultures . . . or that the tribal arts . . . owe anything directly to them.'⁴ I hesitate to accept that conclusion. Ibn Battuta was shocked at how lightly certain aspects of Islam (in regard to the position of women) rested on the Sudanese Moslems, and Persia never gave up its representational art although it adopted Islam. Morocco, much closer, never completely suppressed its arts either. The kingdom, furthermore, included many pagan peoples; Islam was less noticeable below the upper strata of the society—and the king could not suppress the arts of the people, and in fact would be likely to encourage them for the sake of preserving peace and avoiding an upset in political stability (always a delicate balance). The Bambara are a great wood-carving people who have been in the very vortex of the Mali state, and it is difficult for me to see that Islam has had any effect upon their art. Even the suggestion of a tendency to geometrical forms as decorative detail would have to await judgement, because such tendencies can be cited among people far south of the Sudan. None the less, the rulers of Mali, William Fagg comments on my suggestion, were almost certainly anti-art and exerted pressure to relinquish the worship of idols, but perhaps they were not militant in this; yet it is certain that the styles did not 'owe anything' to the rulers.

This clarification explains the apparent contradiction in the caption to Figure 9, where Fagg places his emphasis differently. He says: 'Although nominally Muslim, some Malinké seem to have produced religious sculpture—masks, headdresses and statues, related to Bambara work—until recently.'⁵ Malinké and Mali are in fact the same, the only difference being that the first form we have from the people themselves via French anthropological writers, and the second came through the older Arabic accounts. So the fertility figure of the Malinké that elicited the above caption is in fact something to be associated with the Mali Kingdom. Thus the generalization about the Islamic Sudanese states and art must be taken with qualifications. Where there is a court style, Fagg also informs me, as at Benin, it is different from the tribal style.

Thus we should work with the art forms, as an archaeologist would, by an intimate study of typology and distribution, and we should also watch for relationships with known political entities. The oral traditions of Benin, as mentioned, attested to the radiating artistic influence of Ife. Such influence can travel along trade routes as well as migration paths, and we would hardly expect that all the styles in any particular region would be more closely related to each other than some of them might be to some in other regions. The tendency to divide the continent into art provinces that are purely geographic may be useful for some purposes, but it only obscured whatever historic connexions may exist. The so-called Sudanic, Guinea Coast, and Congo regions, or any other such division, should be ignored for we have ample reason to believe that there were many connexions between the western Sudan and the Forest Belt of the Guinea Coast, and from both to the Congo basin. It is our task to search out by all means available what the specific connexions were, and for this purpose art can be helpful.

One final suggestion on the plastic arts: that two lines of relationship be constantly kept in mind: the relation of a style in a certain material to other styles in that material no matter how distinct geographically; at the same time considering its relationship to styles in other materials and particularly those in the same vicinity.

Now let us turn to the rock-art. It is found in the Sahara, Upper Egypt, the Abyssinian highlands, East and Central Africa, and South Africa. It is scarcely found in the areas where plastic arts are highly developed, and the meaning of this separation, if due to other than environmental factors, requires explanation. Some paintings have been found in Northern Nigeria and perhaps there are others as yet undiscovered which may give them an all-Africa distribution. Could it be that the mural decorations on houses and compound walls were an intermediary connexion between the two? Extremely little recording of such mural styles has ever been done, and much of this neglect cannot now be overcome; but it is something that should receive immediate attention, since what little decoration of such type still exists is fast disappearing.

The rock-paintings of the Sahara, it has been suggested, are related on the one hand to the Eastern Spanish rock-paintings of late palaeolithic age, and on the other to Bushman rock-paintings in southern Africa. If this should turn out to be true, there is a continuum that spans millennia and numerous peoples on two continents; but convergence is just as likely to be the explanation of the similarities.

There are also in the Sahara some items that suggest connexion with Egypt. Two features in paintings of cattle (a kneeling cow, and the representation of the horns front view while the head is side view) may possibly be older than the dynastic period of Egypt, but others (a type of headdress and the 'Uraeus') must be the result of connexions in later dynastic times.

Conrad Kilian once suggested that the history of the Sahara could be divided into a cameline and a pre-cameline period. This was adopted and publicized by Emil Gautier and became widely accepted. On the basis of rock art, we can break up this pre-cameline period into at least three periods. One, a hunting period in which the 'Bubale' was the principal quarry; a pastorial of 'Bovidian' period; and one in which chariots were used. Within the first two periods especially, there are also sub-divisions that can be made on the basis of style, and in many instances a relative chronology can be obtained because some paintings have been superimposed on others, providing thereby a 'stratigraphy'. Further questions of the chronology of this art we will leave to a later chapter.

Since the literature on rock-art is so largely historically oriented, it will not be necessary to discuss it as fully as the plastic arts, but it is to be understood that the same niceties need to be observed in this field as in the other.

AFRICA IN THE ART OF ASIA, THE MIDDLE EAST
AND EUROPE

Berthold Laufer has given us a provocative book entitled *The Giraffe in History and Art* and he has shown that the giraffe, being exclusively an African animal, is an index of connexion with Africa when it appears in the art of other peoples. It in fact is to be found in Indian, Persian, Chinese and medieval European art. These leads are interesting and should be further followed up to determine, as far as possible, the nature and extent of the contact, but this would probably have to be done by literary and/or archaeological means. The art in this instance provided only the fact of historical connexion.

Not only do giraffes appear in Egyptian art, but so do Negroes. Egyptian representations of their southern neighbours should be studied for associated culture traits specifically assigned to them. There will not be many, of course, because they are out of their natural context, but any increment of knowledge is not to be despised. Many of the culture traits of the Egyptians themselves that are so represented show similarities to African materials and practices and would repay study.

The question of racial identification of the human figures, which is not in question in the Egyptian art, is very definitely open to question in the Saharan rock-painting. The arguments of Abbé Breuil and Henri Lhote that the people they call 'Bovidians' were Caucasoid are far from convincing in my opinion and I would leave the question still open.

The existence of the Sahara engravings and paintings, and particularly the charioteers, especially if they were 'Peoples of the Sea' (Lhote) or Cretans (Gsell) rather than the later Garamanteans (who definitely used chariots), raises the question of culture contacts between the western Sudan and the Mediterranean. The time gaps are enormous but some style features, in some media, might survive. Frobenius suggested a palaeo-mediterranean stratum in West African cultures, and although the basis of some of his reasoning must be rejected by us today, we might well reconsider some of the culture traits he indicated. And without too much hope we might attempt to compare some old Mediterranean art styles with African ones. Impressionistically, several things are suggestive. The representation of the face by an inclined plane set at a certain angle to a spindly neck appears in the Ashanti *akua-ba* and in pre-Hellenic Aegean figure. The overall proportions of the figure and the treatment of the hands and feet in bronze figures of the Nuraghi culture of ancient Sardinia and the bronzes of Dahomey have much in common, but the brass work seems to be not more than 150 years old. How could the style, if there is a continuity, have been transmitted? If there was, in fact, any connexion, we have to show not only how the features were diffused, but how they were conserved for so long.

The uses of art in relation to myth have proved useful elsewhere and perhaps might also help in Africa to provide us with further historical inferences, but nothing, so far as I am aware, has ever been attempted on these lines.

Proverbs are represented in Ashanti goldweights and on pot lids made in Cabinda. These make possible an investigation in conjunction with the oral lore. Religious art and ethnography likewise should be studied in co-ordination.

An enormous amount of work can be done in the art field, both to develop a history of art and a history of the art-producing peoples by analyses of their art, but most of this work is still ahead of us.

The exactitude with which place and date are known to the historian is variable; but he always knows that there is both a place and a date, and within limits he always knows what they were; this knowledge being part of the conclusion to which he is led by arguing from the facts before him.

R. G. Collingwood

CHAPTER EIGHT

MEASUREMENTS OF TIME

HISTORY without a time dimension is impossible. We must have a chronology. There are two possibilities: a relative chronology and an absolute chronology. The first merely gives the relative age, i.e. the sequence of events in a series; the second gives us, within certain confined limits, a placement within our sidereal calendrical system.

Historians who work with written documents are used to having large numbers of extremely precise dates, sometimes even to the exact hour of the day, but they also have to deal with some events which are more vaguely related to the time system. Sometimes there are problems of relating one calendar to another, as the Gregorian and the Islamic for which we have a neat formula or the Mayan which is very uncertain.

Pre-historians and proto-historians have often had to be content with relative chronologies which sometimes floated in a limbo between the centuries or even millennia. Lately, however, there has been a considerable advancement in the number and precision of the methods of determining the placement within time of an artifact or an event. Most of these new time-indicating devices or processes bring history into relation to modern physics. Until now, except for wide-ranging archaeology, we have been largely confined to the social sciences (and/or the humanities, depending on how you choose to classify African art and mythology), except for our excursion

into the biological sciences which in itself was not surprising given the biological nature of man. The contributions of physics were somewhat less expected but none the less welcome. They have indeed transformed the whole problem of time-reckoning for us. It is not surprising that the archaeologists, who are not afraid to ask for outside help, have been largely instrumental in bringing about this co-operation, but a good part of it also rests upon new discoveries by physicists.

The first of these startling methods was that of Carbon fourteen (C14), which was one of the happier by-products of nuclear research. It depends on the even rate of disintegration of an isotope of carbon found in living matter. This degeneration begins at the death of the plant or animal. Most parts of the dead plant or animal will quickly decompose, but wood (or charcoal) and bones may persist in favourable conditions for a very long time. The use of bones is presenting some difficulties that are not as yet worked out, and dates from the two different materials do not seem to equate as they should; but the solution of this problem will probably soon be obtained. Most of our dates so far have been obtained from wood or charcoal. These have given us the most precise dates in pre-history, except where inscriptions have been found. Not all of the 'bugs' are worked out yet, and some authorities are saying that we ought to have a little more caution than was common in the first flush of enthusiasm over this wonderful tool. Even so, it remains unparalleled in its field.

It is a pity that the other applications of nuclear research should make possible the large-scale destruction of the evidence C14 can give us. The explosion of atomic bombs, even in testing, makes impossible the use of this method over a wide area. Thus not only in the name of the future but also in the name of the past should we protest the use of these horrible and inhuman engines no matter who uses them, and the recent explosions of nuclear devices in the Sahara are greatly to be regretted in terms of African history. These explosions were in the very region in which we might have hoped to find evidence of the time of early trans-saharan contacts.

Before the advent of C14, archaeologists had as their main reliance, stratigraphy. This only gave a relative chronology, those things that were deeper in the earth being older than those above them in the same soil. Geologists can tell ages of some earth strata but they cannot work on such a small scale as is necessary in human history. It would be like trying to use a yard-stick when a micrometer was needed.

Fluorine tests are useful, particularly where there may have been some disturbance of the soil, as they could tell whether two pieces of bone had been in the same strata the same length of time, and are an additional check on the stratigraphy in any case.

In northern Europe, particularly in previously glaciated areas, a study of varves in the soil deposited in lakes showed the pattern of annual accretion, and this is now established with considerable precision for Scandinavia for a period of about ten millennia. Objects that can be related to a varve can be dated, and by extension other cultural materials related to the original object can be assigned an equivalent date. North American varves have been studied, and it is claimed that they correlate with those of Europe, but this is still questioned. Varves elsewhere are more uncertain until more work has been done on them. Thus far, only in East Africa has this possibility been investigated, and the results are still uncertain. The tropics in general seem less promising for this method than the colder parts of the world.

Dendrochronology, or the counting of tree rings, has also proved useful in the northern temperate zone. But this method also depends on an annual rotation of seasons and would be useless in the tropical rain forest (but very little wood survives long there anyway); that it might be applicable in regions where the rain system is such that there is an alternation of a rapid growing season with a period of quiescence (i.e. a wet and a dry season), is indicated by a count made on a wooden lintel from Zimbabwe. This particular wood, however, exudes a poisonous substance and so is not used until thoroughly dried out, and it has been suggested that this particular lintel might have been made when the tree had already been dead for some centuries!

Since C14 began the new phase in more hopeful dating techniques, others have been added. The archaeomagnetic test is a very promising one because it can date pot sherds, the most common cultural material retrieved on most sites. When the pot was 'fired', whether in a kiln or not, it had to be brought up to a certain temperature for the clay to be transformed into ceramic. When the cooling object passes through a critical temperature, the magnetic characteristics of its locality and time are fixed in it. Since these characteristics of magnetism are constantly changing at a known, steady rate, it is now possible to determine how long ago the pot was made.

Fortunately, pots are fragile and frequently broken in use. So the sherd would not likely be older than other artifacts in the same strata. Also pots are not usually easily transportable and so were probably made in the area where found. Thus their date can be calculated by that locality's magnetic scheme. We do know a few instances in which pots were carried over great distances but these were special cases. For example, the early Greeks shipped wine and oil in amphorae by sea and up rivers so that Greek pottery has been found far up the Rhone in France. Usually, however, we could expect pots to be much closer to home.

Since pots are not fixed to the earth, only the intensity of magnetism can be used in determining the age of a pot sherd, but the kiln, if one was used, or the earthen floor or the wall of a pisé house of which the thatch roof and timbers were burned can be tested for both intensity and direction of magnetism.

The hindrance in the use of this method is that the schema of each region's changing regimen of magnetism must be worked out before the sherds or kilns can be tested. This has been done for England and Greece but not yet for Africa.

Like C_{14}, this test is impossible after an atomic explosion.

A test on glass has been announced which consists of the counting of microscopic flakings of the surface. It was found that Roman glass of known date gave the correct results by this method. Like the dendrochronology, this depends on annual variation of seasons, but in this case the important factor is succession of a period of cold by one of warmth. There is not much glass, earlier than European contact, likely to be found in Africa, but if it should be, the applicability of this test in tropical regions would still have to be determined.

Even if the latter test is useless for African chronologies, it is part of the exciting development in physics which will probably continue to offer us as yet unexpected possibilities for precision in dating the past.

It would not be possible to review here all the techniques being developed in physics, geology, astronomy and oceanography that provide archaeologists with time correlations. In addition, archaeology has from cultural materials some other old stand-bys of dating, but they are not always present in Africa. First, is inscriptions. This has been of such importance in Mesopotamia as to put these sites in a class by themselves, but elsewhere is of varying importance. In Africa we need not expect too much but we have undoubtedly not exhausted all the sites with inscriptions of some type; but on this continent they are apt to present particular difficulties, e.g. Meroëtic and Tifenath. Secondly, numismatics. There is scarcely a better time-marker than a known system of coinage. Coins are not common in Africa, but within reach of the northern and eastern coast they are possibilities. Coins have been found in West Africa as far south as the Niger River and in East Africa, coins are found not only singly but even in hoards. Finally, imports. Dateable trade items can be of as much importance as coins. In East Africa, Chinese porcelain (which is dateable by its style) is so common as an import in late pre-European periods that Sir Mortimer Wheeler said the pre-history of East Africa would be written in porcelain. Beads have an importance over a wider area and longer time, but identification of origin is not always as easy as with the porcelain.

Each of the other approaches to pre-history has its own dating problems, but none is in quite so favourable a position as archaeology.

Oral traditions are usually undateable. Sometimes, however, there are references in the traditions that can be dated. It might be an event that is attested by another source, perhaps even written, and can then be raised out of timelessness. Or there might be a reference to an eclipse. B. Davidson has dramatized the Bashongo eclipse more than E. Torday, who recorded it, did; but unless there are many more, this is not a method, despite Davidson's hallelujahs, but an unusual case. How many more such are there? It is hard to tell. Perhaps not many, but a number of other cases are known.

Genealogies given in traditions are, on the other hand,

rather common. If it is a true genealogy, then enough years must elapse between each individual for the new offspring to mature sufficiently to reproduce. Biologically, this would be just after puberty, but in human societies non-biological factors intervene and the age at marriage will be somewhat, and often considerably, beyond puberty. How many years then should we allow for a generation? Estimates vary from 30 to 17. Thus, by taking the smaller number one might get an age for a genealogical line almost twice as long as that calculated by the larger figure.

Sometimes we get a series of names that are not in a genealogical relationship but are successors to an office—a list of kings or chiefs or 'queen-mothers'. We have the actual names in the case of the Baganda, but only the number in the case of Old Ghana. How do we arrive at an average length of reign? There is a minimum figure below which we could not calculate a generation, but there is no such limitation on a reign; some kings last in office only a matter of months. On the other hand, it is more difficult to fix a maximum length to a reign than to a generation. No new king can succeed so long as the old one continues to reign, and if one is long-lived (and there are no restrictions on aged rulers such as may be the case with 'divine-kings'), then a reign of eighty years is not impossible. Some of that length are on record. With the calculation of generation, however, it makes no difference (in the calculation) how long the parent continues to live after the offspring has been born.

The best way to arrive at a figure to use in calculating the length of time involved in either type of list is to take known cases (as many as can be found) and see what the maxima and minima and averages are. In doing this, we should also be alert to any conditions of society which might affect the particular case. If we can feel reasonably sure that some condition does affect the length of a generation or a reign, we would then not use the average but modify it. In doing this, we would be guided by the maxima and minima in deciding how far in either way the modification should go. Of course, it will still be an estimate, but one more carefully arrived at.

Myths found among African people may be recognizable as recorded myths of Mediterranean or Asian peoples, and therefore of at least the age of the recorded non-African version. This does tell us something of the antiquity of the myth, but it doesn't tell us anything about how long the African people under consideration have had it nor how they came to have it. Myths may be older than the society that holds them. The Ashanti, for example, formed as an *Oman*, or state, at the end of the seventeenth century, have beliefs that are far older. The constituent peoples who went into the formation of the Ashanti brought with them, probably to some extent from divergent sources, the beliefs that were fused together when the peoples themselves were fused. Thus one cannot use myth as an indicator of antiquity of the political entirety.

John Fisher has suggested that the variations in folk tales among cognate peoples may give a suggestion of the age of the tale. He analyses the tales into units and compares the units among cognate peoples for the extent of modification. The direction of modification may also, he suggests, tell us something about the kind of culture change that has occurred.

Edward Sapir, in a brilliant essay, 'Time-Perspective in Aboriginal American Indian Societies' outlined ways in which linguistics affords relative ages for the culture items that words refer to. Obsolete forms, such as the inflexion in ox-oxen, indicate that the animal was known to English speakers when that inflexion was the common way of forming plurals. The elaboration of terms, also, to keep the example in the same area, such as heifer, calf, cow, cattle, ox, etc. indicate that the culture-complex is not new.

A number of such indices can give us some idea of age and tell us that a trait is, say, older than a certain linguistic change, but this is not an absolute chronology.

Morris Swadesh, once a student of Sapir, has carried the task to a closer precision. He argues that the rate of linguistic differentiation is sufficiently regular so that one can calculate to within about two centuries per millennium the time required for the divergence between any two related languages. This technique of 'glotto-chronology' has been tested on some languages where the time depth is known; but that the method can be relied upon in other cases is not beyond controversy. A sympathetic discussion of the problems involved is Dell

Hymes' article 'Lexico-statistics thus far' in *Current Anthropology*, and I refer you to this for details.

If this method proves itself, it will be an enormous boon to historical studies. Meanwhile, it should be tried out on every possible occasion, for only in this way will we accumulate enough cases to make an extensive assessment of the procedure and so be able to end the controversy—one way or the other. My own inclination is that it will stand—perhaps at worst only as a rough calculation rather than a really absolute chronological device—but some refinements, at best, will be needed.

Ethnology, like linguistics, has used the degree of elaboration to indicate age of a culture-complex. It has also used the geographical extension of a trait or complex to indicate age. In both instances, the assumption is that time is required for elaboration and diffusion. Both of these indices give only a relative chronology, and ethnology has so far been unable to put forward a means of determining absolute time, and perhaps is unlikely to do so.

Ethno-botany and ethno-zoology have no absolute time markers either, except in the case of dated entries, e.g. the American plants, peanuts and manioc introduced to Africa. This gives a *terminus ad quem* in studying the diffusion into particular areas within the continent.

Sir Harry Johnston thought he had such a case because he knew the time the chicken arrived in Egypt from records of that country and assumed that the bird must have diffused from there southward; and since he found the cognate terms for chicken widely spread in Bantu languages he thought that he could calculate the age of the proto-Bantu by the Egyptian date. Unfortunately, it is not at all certain, in fact most unlikely, that the chicken reached the Bantu speakers from Egypt, but it seems more probable that it came in directly from the East African coast.

Variation is, like linguistic and ethnologic elaborations, a process that takes time. F. Irvine says that there are about 200 varieties of yams in West Africa and this certainly argues long cultivation of the plant in that area. How long? Could an attempt be made to formulate an analogy of glotto-chronology —a 'cultivar-chronology'—to make this more precise? Many botanists argue that the farming techniques (and the propensities of the cultivators), the genetic composition of the plant, and the edapic and ecological conditions may influence the rate of variation. None the less, the problem deserves further study.

The rock-paintings have received a good deal of attention in terms of their age. Relative age of individual figures can be observed when one has been superimposed upon another. This 'palimpsest' gives a 'stratigraphy'. With an analysis of styles, we can then assign relative ages not just to individual figures, but to styles.

Hopes have been put forward that age could be determined by the degree of patination of the surface of the rock. However, the local climatic conditions affect the rate at which the patina is formed. The obelisk known as Cleopatra's Needle has weathered more since it was brought to London only a little over a century ago than it had done in millennia in Egypt. Perhaps comparisons of one local piece with another may be possible if the glass-patina experience could be extended to this material, but a general system of time-determination by a study of patina seems out of the question. The question of rate of colour loss comes down to the same thing.

Associated finds, however, can date paintings. Excavating at the base of the rock, the colour pigments have been found, in some instances; and since some colours are characteristic of certain styles, and other colours of other styles, it is possible to give the sequence of the styles by the stratigraphy of the painter's lost supplies of pigment. Sometimes stone tools are found with the pigment and so the painting can be associated with an actual culture.

Thus all the means of investigating the past, archaeology, oral traditions, linguistics, ethnology, ethno-botany and art, have all their peculiar problems with chronology. Of these, only archaeology is well on the way to certainty, with, perhaps, linguistics next in line. This is the same order that we found for the degree of development of their methodology. Perhaps, then, as the other approaches to the past refine their procedures, there will emerge better chronological indicators. This is not too much to hope for, seeing the progress that has been made in several facets of historical reconstruction in recent decades.

We can assume that this improvement of our understanding will continue.

Nothing is more crucial than that we should improve our means of assigning events, cultures, artifacts, traits, etc. to a time period. We want to know not only what happened and where it happened and to whom, but also when it happened. If we do not know when the various cultures flourished, how can we determine what relationships there may have been between them?

Time is the essence of history; it is therefore essential that we perfect our chronology.

History is the attempt to fuse together these *disjecta membra*, the scattered limbs of the past and to synthesize them and mold them in new shape.

Ernst Cassirer

CHAPTER NINE

PROCESS IN NATURE, SOCIETY AND HISTORY

What is Process? Some of the older sociologists, e.g. Cooley, wrote extensively about 'social process'. The term is not today in the forefront of sociological discussion. 'Function', while not exactly a synonym, has pre-empted some of the ground of the older term. 'Social Action' as used by Talcott Parsons, which is a very inclusive term, subsumes 'process'.

Any attempt to define it briefly here will inevitably result in simplification, so I will merely say that I wish to indicate by the term: (1) all social interchange within a (more or less) stable society, and (2) changes in the patterns of the society.

I prefer the word process in this context for a number of reasons; it is not exclusively associated with a particular school of sociology and, especially, because the same word can be used to refer not only to the working of the social organism, but also to the working of the ecological system.

Relation of Process to History. History is an account of human activities through time in a social and natural environment. Process is in relationship with each of these dimensions of human activities. History does not occur in a vacuum; each act in the historical drama has a certain stage and a particular setting, as well as actors of a certain characterization together with their actions. That an understanding of the natural and social sciences can be helpful in comprehending and interpreting an historic event in its fullest context does not, I hope, need to be laboured. But we can go further and say that process is essentially historical, in that history is predicated upon a

time-dimension, and time is a measure of change while process is patterned change.

Processual Reasoning. The scholar who attempts to reconstruct the African past must be competent in the techniques necessary for the accumulation of the data; but he must then set his data in relationships which will be only as creditable as his mastery of the natural and social processes that are involved in his formulation. The standards of creditability vary from one generation of historians to the next and tend to become more stringent as knowledge of natural and social process grows. It is true that there has generally been a slight hiatus between what passes as believable and plausible among historians and among social and/or natural scientists of the same generation. That is, the historian, giving his main attention elsewhere, is usually not familiar with the latest advances in the conceptualization of process, and often relies on what he has picked up in his general education. This means that in his mature years he is still using standards of credibility that he acquired as a young scholar. It is important that an historian spend his years of study not merely collecting more facts, but also improving his means of interpreting them. This is applicable to any field of history, although it may be less obvious in well-cultivated fields; but in reconstruction from unwritten sources the problems of process are more in the forefront and need constantly to be faced. Comprehension comes gradually from wide reading of history, anthropology and other natural and social sciences, but better than waiting to absorb as by osmosis such an understanding, it would be better to pursue the study of process.

Let us take an example of bad processual reasoning. We can find a number of them in Balmer's *History of the Akan Peoples*. Balmer views the grasslands as corridors stretching from east to west across the continent, and also from north to south on the eastern side of Africa; and he imagines that 'the first Negro people entered Africa or took their rise in the lands near the river Nile and settled at that end of the Sudan'. At the time he was writing, nearly everyone who had expressed an opinion thought of Asia as being the homeland of mankind and so the problem was to explain how the Negro arrived in Africa. Maurice Delafosse was of a similar opinion, and Grandidier had an even more fantastic opinion that the Negro was brought from Melanesia by the ancestors of the Malayo-Polynesian-speaking ancestors of the Malagesy of Madagascar! Balmer's position on this point is not unreasonable in light of the state of knowledge of his time, although we might today be more inclined to believe that the Negro developed in Africa rather than coming from elsewhere.

This grouping of Negro people in north-eastern Africa was forced to disperse, as Balmer visualizes it, by famines, invasions of other peoples, and wars.

The movement of the people is supposed to have turned in two directions, one southwards by way of the great lakes and the east coast, the other westward by way of the wide strip of land which we have described as a corridor and now known as the Sudan. The people who turned southward afterwards came to be known as the Bantus, one of the great divisions of the African people. The similarity of the words Bantu and Fanti may not be without significance.[1]

This last suggestion would no doubt have been surprising to W. H. I. Bleek, who coined the word Bantu; and no African people ever called themselves that, not at least until after it had been applied to them by Europeans.

In regard to the peoples of Guinea and the western Sudan we are then told that 'so unceasing and overpowering was the pressure, so numerous were their foes that in the end they had to give way and flee towards the west'. The process sorted out the strong from the weak:

In the warfare their strongest and most intelligent men would be slain for they would fight the hardest, and most daringly, and their finest women would be taken captives. Only the weakest would be left to escape, and that is the reason why so many of the people who live in out-of-the-way parts of the Atlantic coast are so poor and undeveloped. All the spirit was crushed out of them in the course of their long wanderings and fightings across the Sudan.[2]

It is perhaps of some interest to note that Balmer, in this passage, views human nature as unvariable, an entity not affected by cultural values, which therefore he can judge by his knowledge of his own people, whom he mistakes for common humanity, when it is in fact only one of its variants: European culture. In reality, many peoples, in Africa and elsewhere, do not share the European values of chivalrous valour. They prefer to gain their victories by crafty means rather than unduly risking bodily harm which they would view as foolhardy. In such a case the most intelligent men would not fight 'most daringly' but most slyly. Although one is not justified on the basis of present knowledge in asserting how or if they fought, some Africans may indeed have fought in the manner Balmer visualized, yet even then the consequences need not necessarily have resulted in a concentration of (the genes of?) weakness in certain populations, for defeated peoples combined with their conquerors perhaps as often as they fled from them. Also the weakness is not in the people themselves but in their means of warfare, and these can be borrowed from the enemy; and imitation in warfare was very common. Balmer perhaps got the idea from Lady Lugard.[3]

We can take another instance from the same author:

It was because, in the past, the Negro people of the Sudan made slaves of each other that they lost their strength and became dis-united and weak as a nation.[4]

And it was the continuation of this custom that was to be the undoing of the Ashantis, who had

the power to combine and by so doing they acquired political strength and were able to extend their power and, in a measure, create an empire. Had they been truly wise they might have been able to restore the position of the ancient kingdom of Ghana with themselves as a new center. Unhappily they retained the ancient habit of making slaves.[5]

Balmer partly absolves the West Africans for their part in this practice.

They were not altogether to blame for this as the custom of making slaves is a very old one, and has been practised by nations of much greater knowledge and power than the Negroes, especially by those who lived in the north and east of Africa, to whom the peoples of the Sudan naturally looked for guidance . . .[6]

Thus the blame can be laid at the door of Islam, according to the Rev. Balmer, for

this religion which Africans have respected so much has always tolerated the habit of making slaves and it is no doubt from them that the Negroes learnt the fatal custom. Wherever it has been allowed, the people who practised it have, in time, gone down in power, wealth and learning, and the chief reason for the decay has been the custom of making slaves.[7]

How this can be said with a straight face when his country had made itself rich, in no small measure, on the slave trade is a problem for the psychologist rather than for us here. Differences in fire power, organization of military supplies, and such factors are ignored by the reverend historian so that he can blame a factor he abhorred.

Perhaps the example of bad processual reasoning that has most bedevilled African history is C. G. Seligman's Hamitic Hypothesis:

... the civilizations of Africa are the civilizations of the Hamites, its history the record of these peoples and of their interaction with the other two African stocks, the Negro and the Bushman ...

The incoming Hamites were pastoral 'Europeans'—arriving wave after wave—better armed as well as quicker-witted than the dark agricultural Negroes, for it must be remembered that there was no Bronze Age in Africa, and we may believe that the Negro, who is now an excellent iron-worker, learnt this art from the Hamite. Diagrammatically the process may be described as follows. At first the Hamites, or at least their aristocracy would endeavour to marry Hamitic women, but it cannot have been long before a series of peoples combining Negro and Hamitic blood arose; these, superior to the true Negro, would be regarded with disdain by the next incoming wave of Hamites and be pushed farther inland to play the part of an incoming aristocracy *vis à vis* the Negroes on whom they impinged. And this process was repeated with minor modifications over a very long period of time, the pastoralists always asserting their superiority over the agriculturalists, who constantly tended to leave their mode of life or at least to combine it with the latter.[8]

Seligman assumed, as did many of his generation and, more lamentably, many of his later followers, that the Hamitic-speaking peoples, if they resembled him in complexion must feel as he did about race and would immediately and 'naturally' react towards the dark skin as a sign of inferiority. He took for granted that in the past, as in the colonial period in which he flourished, the white would inevitably dominate the black. He was ignorant of African history or he would have known, as Ibn Khaldun tells us, that black kings of the Western Sudan were at times sovereign over the Berbers of the desert. He is still more culpable when it comes to his own discipline; though an anthropologist, he did not know what is axiomatic in his field, that ability cannot be related to races but only to individuals. While some Europeans may be 'quicker-witted' than some Negroes, conversely, it is equally true that some Negroes are 'quicker-witted' than some Europeans. Aristocracies would not therefore depend upon the percentage of white ancestry (assuming as he does that quick-wittedness is a factor in establishing this stratification) but able individuals occurring randomly in both the white and black and mixed populations would be equally active (if cultural values, which he here ignores, could for the moment be assumed to be unimportant) in so asserting themselves. It was Negro and *métisé* individuals of ability, power and culture, representing the then flourishing civilization of Islam, in comparison to which medieval Spain was barbaric, that, according to Gilberto Frerre, impressed upon the Iberian a still palpable admiration for the dark *moreno* and *morena* type.

Seligman equates his Hamites and pastoralists, and thus confuses de Gobineau and Franz Oppenheim. The latter theorized that the state arose through the conquest of agriculturalists by pastoralists, and his was not a racist interpretation but a cultural one: the pastoralists, he claimed, were better organized for mobility, and therefore military strategy, than the agriculturalists, and he was concerned only with explaining how an autocratic state could arise from what he postulated as 'primitive democracy'. Ratzel had accumulated a number of cases which seemed to support this idea, but there are other cases when the pastoralists streaming out of a drought-stricken steppe into a strongly organized arable area beg the agriculturalists for hospitality and wish to be permitted to work as menials for their sustenance.

This 'Hamitic Hypothesis' is thus undermined by the fact that not only has the Negro sometimes dominated the white, but that the agriculturalist has sometimes dominated the pastoralist. Seligman's interpretation is today in most places thoroughly discredited, yet strangely his book was recently reprinted with no important revision. Yet we must not push the pendulum too far the other way and deny the Hamitic-speaking peoples and/or the African Caucasoids any share in African history. They have been a factor, and in some instances an important one, but they have not been as all-pervasive as has for so long been imagined.

We must today be more conscious of process and, of course, good historians have generally been so. But greater emphasis can now be put on process. F. J. Teggart says:

We are now in a position to recognize the nature of the processes which have been operative throughout human history . . . It opens up new fields of inquiry for historical investigation.[9]

Let us now consider a few significant processes.

NATURAL PROCESS

We need to know what kind of a physical world a people lived in and this cannot always be assumed to be the same as that of the present day. Climatic change has affected many parts of Africa in the period of man's habitation there. The Western Sahara was once more widely habitable; the desert is still encroaching southward upon the Sahel which in turn invades the grasslands; further south, the forests are retreating, but here the human factor is more important than the climatic. It is possible to reconstruct former climates, and when we have done that to determine the kind of ecology in which the people at that time had to live, and the eco-system, whatever it may have been, permits a certain variety of adaptations and rules out others. By examining our evidence within this framework, we can make deductions concerning their economy. Sometimes our data on the economy itself may be evidence for the climate, e.g. bones of domestic animals or rock paintings of them tell us not only that the people were stock raisers but that the ecology permitted it at that time. The economy is functionally inter-twined with the social organization, and although we cannot tell from it all facets of the social structure, we will at least be able to obtain a general outline. Thus we progress in under-standing that continuum that Daryll Forde has called Habitat, Economy and Society.

Some questions we need to ask under this heading: What is (or was) the climate? For a hunting people, what game exists in the eco-system and what are its habits? For a farming people, what crops will grow (and which will not), and what kind of care do they require? What parasites and diseases affect the animals and/or crops on which the group depends; which affect the people themselves; and what are the manifestations of these afflictions? Is the uncultivated vegetation at a climax or subclimax? Why? What kinds of economy were possible in the given ecology? What influence would the ecology and economy have upon the social organization?

For the investigation of the previous conditions of the environment, we have a number of specialized sciences.

Palaeoclimatology. This yields us information from the kinds of soils laid down, since each is created under certain meteorological conditions. We can extrapolate solar radiation variations from astronomy and the study of tree rings. Fossils tell us what kinds of life were possible and therefore the climatic conditions in which they lived.

Palaeobotany. Pollens, grains and sometimes whole plants unearthed in soil strata tell us what the vegetation was at the given period.

Palaeogeography. We are able to discover from raised and sunken coasts, old lake-beds, altered river courses and dried-up marshes that the features of the landscape were significantly different at certain periods for the inhabitants.

Palaeontology brings us information on the physical types of man with which we are dealing.

Several of these palaeo-sciences except the last commonly deal with such long time-spans that they ante-date the arrival of mankind, and it is not always easy to extract from the specialists the restricted information we may need. Nor are they exactly accurate in detail, but co-operation can and should be developed.

SOCIAL PROCESS

Any social process may be important at some point, but some of the social processes are more commonly faced than others by historians in Africa.

Migration. This usually occurs by small numbers of people filtering slowly into an area, and perhaps then followed by larger numbers in a more organized fashion. The latter stage is more easily recognized than the former, but the earlier arrivals may be important in the overall movement. Transhumance, or seasonal wandering with flocks or herds, and shifting agriculture are specific varieties of migration which may, but need not, go through both the phases outlined above. Small armed bands, sometimes without women of their own group, sometimes appear as marauders and remain as conquerors, and occasionally a whole society is impelled to go on the march in search of a new home. It is important in considering newcomers into an area to try to determine what kind of migratory process was involved.

Political Organization. There has been so much talk of 'kinship societies' that even anthropologists are often confused about the reality behind the term. I. Schapera[10] has demonstrated that a tribe is a political entity and not a kinship grouping. Evans-Pritchard had prepared the way by noting that political meaning was expressed in a kinship 'idiom'. This leads us to a related process.

State Formation. Much controversy has centred on the question of the provenience of states. Pallotini cogently discusses the Etruscan case. Some held it came from Asia Minor; some from the Danube valley. Pallotini, taking France as an analogy, showed that contributions to the individuality of the state may come from various places, but it is not necessary to postulate that the state itself was brought in from outside. If this holds for Etruria, it probably does for most of Africa as well. Though Axum may have been transplanted from South Arabia, most African states are likely to have been formed in their own locale—but not necessarily without the stimulus of ideas from one or more state-building peoples, usually in some other part of Africa, although in some instances from outside the continent.

Diffusion. The process of the spread of ideas has been used in the past to explain too much, too simply. But diffusion does occur and we cannot disregard it even if we do reject the formulations of some diffusionists. The concept of acculturation is a major addition to our understanding of diffusion; a thing borrowed is always altered in some way to fit into the borrowing cultural system.

Trade. Trade is one of the most efficacious vehicles of diffusion. Trade is of great antiquity, attested in the Palaeolithic by seashells found far inland and by wide distribution of flints of a specific local provenience. Trade is necessary to settled, civilized life and increases proportionately. There is trade between cultural equals which results in products of one culture being found in the remains of another, and this has been very helpful to archaeologists. Trade between unequals—perhaps of the silent barter type—may be less evident, as the more developed peoples are gathering raw materials, and the less developed peoples are often satisfied with perishables such as textiles and strong drink. K. Polanyi suggests that in ancient times, all trade was 'administered' or controlled by the state. One of his case studies was Dahomey.

War. Another mechanism of diffusion is war. Through the taking of booty, the material culture of two warring groups becomes more similar. It is more incumbent upon us to study our enemies than our friends because such knowledge may lead to victory—but it may also lead to imitation. However, the need to distinguish friends from enemies lends emphasis to some distinguishing trait; and imitation, aside from warfare techniques, cannot be anywhere near complete.

Industrial Processes. The manufacture and use of iron has been widely diffused in Africa; the use more widely than the manufacture. Iron smelting, claimed by some to have originated in Africa, was more likely introduced from elsewhere and probably by more than one route. Iron has had tremendous social consequences. Probably all of the African states except in the Nile valley are iron age in their origins; weapons of this metal, in other words, have been as important to the Bakuba as to the Hittites. The smith frequently has a special position in society, either as a sorcerer or as a separate (and sometimes despised) endogamous caste. The traditions of some ruling lineages go back to founders who were smiths.

Urbanization. Many people think that there were no cities in pre-European Africa, but this is not true. Kumbi, Walata, Timbuctu, Gao, Kano, Oyo, Benin, Mbanza (San Salvador), Zimbabwe, Sofala, Kilwa, Mombasa, Malindi, Axum, Napata are only the most obvious of the old African cities. The urban revolution followed in its spread upon its pre-requisite, the Neolithic. It involves a development of the social divison of labour, and complexity of social structure, resulting perhaps in some form of social stratification. Urbanization is intimately related to state-formation.

Ritual. The role of ritual in social life can be traced in all aspects of the society, in the religion, the court, the family, and in relations with outsiders. Since ritual has been touched on in another part of this book, we will not enter into a discussion of it here.

Social and Cultural Change. Innovation (i.e. invention) or borrowing will account for most of the change in societies, but each case occurs in a number of different ways. Sudden changes (revolutions) are always matters of great historical interest. In what did the change consist? What brought about the change? Why did it happen so fast? On the other hand, customs sometimes persist after they are no longer efficacious. This has been called *ossification* by some sociologists and considered to be a common tendency in human societies.

Ideal Types. After a study of many variants of an institution, one comes to know the model form and something of the frequency of the variations. The importance of the model form, called an ideal-type by Max Weber, for sociological generalization is well known. Can it be useful to the historian when he is not in search of a generalization but in elucidation of a specific instance of past action? It can; but of course there is a difference, for whereas in sociological generalization one can, for the moment, forget the variability behind the ideal type, in processual reasoning in historical reconstruction, however, one would never want to get out of sight of the variants. That is to say, the ideal type is a handy device for a first check on the likely functioning of a character in an oral tradition or of the use to which an excavated artifact may have been put, but one would also want to consider the possibility of other behavioural patterns within the known range.

Many historical questions in Africa still pose us problems of process. Did the expansion of the Bantu-speaking peoples occur because of the acquisition of new food crops that resulted in population expansion, or did the expansion come about because they acquired superior technology, e.g. iron, which permitted them to forge better weapons and overpower the former occupants of the land? There are states in the western Sudan and states in the Guinea coast forests and the former seem to be older than the latter; are the forest states offshoots of the grassland, and if so, how were they effectuated?

The treatment of social and natural process requires more than the casual attention of the historian who is engaged in historical reconstruction. This is a subject which should be given as close study as the various means of obtaining the data which now, through processual reasoning, are to be put into meaningful relationships.

The enlargement of historical knowledge comes about mainly through finding how to use as evidence this or that kind of perceived fact which historians have hitherto thought useless to them. The whole perceptible world, then, is potentially and in principle evidence to the historian. It becomes actual evidence in so far as he can use it.

R. G. Collingwood

CHAPTER TEN

NEW STRATEGIES OF HISTORY

So many and varied things have been touched on that it has been impossible to avoid creating an impression of chaos. In order to dispel this chaos, we must have organization, and to meet problems of this scale, I think you will agree, it must be a very good organization.

Archaeology, linguistics and other disciplines related to history has each its own strategy. Some of these are now quite well developed; some need much, much more refinement.

A methodology of historical reconstruction, however, must be more than a collection of methods; it must provide a synthesis of all the individual methods. This involves not only determining the inter-relationships between different classes of data, but the problem of weighing one set of data against another in the same class, or of one class against another. As we have concentrated our attention on the unwritten sources, we must not forget, at this point, that there is the necessity of bringing these materials into relationship with archival materials.

Ideally, each strategy should be kept distinct and unconfused by data proper to other strategies, until the selected line of investigation has been completed. To introduce a linguistic datum into an ethnobotanical research, except as a footnote for later investigation, is to risk a false illusion of confirmation. This can disguise a weakness of the ethnobotanical data, while the linguistic datum is out of context and therefore of uncertain validity.

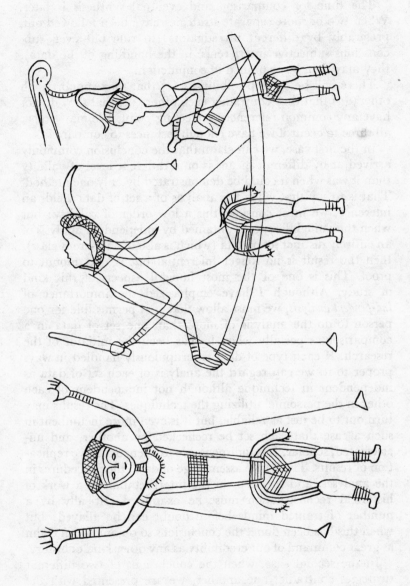

The time for comparison and eventual synthesis is later. When two or more separate strategies have been followed out, preferably by different investigators (to rule out even sub-conscious subjective interference in the handling of the data), they may then be examined in conjunction.

There will be three possibilities: (1) that they support each other; (2) that they contradict each other; (3) that they do not have any common reference or meeting point. We may expect all three to occur if we have enough instances to compare.

In the first case, we can claim that the conclusion commonly arrived at by different means is on a different level of validity than it was when it could be demonstrated by only one method. That is to say that when the analysis of a set of data yields an inference, we must consider this a low order of validity; but when the same inference is obtained by independent analysis of an entirely distinct set of data (which is also of a different class), then the result is no longer inferential but is tantamount to proof. This is one of the most hopeful aspects of this kind of study. Although I have emphasized the importance of *independent analysis*, we must allow that it is permissible for one person to do the analysis of more than one set of data in a comparison, especially when he has been the initiator of the research. If each type of data is scrupulously handled in ways proper to it, we can regard the analysis of each set of data as independent in technique although not independent of each other in the personnel utilizing the techniques. The results may turn out to be just as reliable, but it is even more incumbent in such a case that each set be rechecked by another, and un-associated, scholar. It is indispensable to science to have replication of results. The whole assemblage of data, the procedures in the analyses, and the steps in the interpretation of a work of historical reconstruction must be examined critically by a number of trained minds before doubt can be allayed; but when this has been done, the conclusions so obtained can claim as great command of our credibility as any other kind of history.

In the second case, when the conclusions of two different strategies contradict one another, we are presented with the question not only of the validity of the particular conclusions, but of the reliability of our strategies. The question of relia-bility of the strategy is the more important. Most of our procedures are in need of improvement, and all are susceptible to further refinement. The pitting of one strategy against another may help to show us the weaknesses and lead to the development of more reliable procedures. Thus, these instances of contradiction are not lightly to be considered failures and thrown in the waste-basket; they should become objects of study for the methodologists.

Sometimes, however, the strategy may not be in question. It may be that the set of data in one approach was extensive and detailed and the set of data in the other was scanty or in some way defective. Tentatively, at least, we would lean on the conclusion from the more complete set of data. But if no distinction can be made on the quality of the raw data, we may still be able to assign a greater weight to one strategy than to another. As indicated earlier, archaeology and linguistics have more rigorous strategies than oral tradition or art. In general, then, we would place our reliability, in case of a contradiction, on the stronger strategy. In some instances, however, the data in the weaker strategy may be of a pertinence that, in the problem concerned, exceeds that of the alternate strategy. We would then not be able to make an easy decision; but consideration of these cases will gradually increase our comprehension of the problems implicit in methodology and will also lead to greater control of the variables involved.

The third case, in which the conclusions do not have any common ground, we must expect to be all too common. It may be that the time-depth is different, so that there can be no contact because of the time-gap between the different periods. It may be that the conclusions refer to different aspects of the society, so that there could only be a rather vague check of functional compatibility; but this could be so wide as to be of little significance. If more data can be obtained, it may be possible to supplement one or the other pieces of research so that it extends into an area where comparison is then possible, and the instance is transferred to either the first or the second case.

In the first case, we may consider the different strategies as complementary. They support each other, and they extend, in conjunction, the area of our knowledge. They co-ordinate; they form a composite. In the second case, we may consider the different strategies as competing. Each is on trial with the other as judge. Both senses are important to the furtherance of our knowledge of the past.

The foregoing is a logical construction. It was prefaced by the word, *ideally*. The complete separation of strategies is not, in all instances, possible. It is part of the strategy of archaeology to use oral tradition and anthropology in its interpretation of artifacts. The linguistic analysis of terms is a proper part of the strategy of oral tradition. And there are other overlappings. It would be foolish to try to be such a purist that we would expunge such tried and useful combinations; but where later comparisons are to be made, we must avoid a double use of the same data. It must not appear on both sides and be counted as a concurrence, for it was, to begin with, identical.

The occasional use of outside materials or procedures in a strategy does not invalidate all later comparative study; it merely calls for careful accounting.

The word strategy, as used above, is based on the assumption that data can be put in certain classes so that the items in each class will have a more intimate relationship to each other than to those in another class. This is the basis upon which our scholarly disciplines are founded. They have been called disciplines because training is required in an efficacious pursuit of the study. Training takes considerable time. It is thus not easy to master several disciplines. How then can co-ordinated multi-disciplinary research be achieved? Let us consider various ways.

We can take an analogy from movie-making. A Charlie Chaplin or a Sacha Guitry can write the scenario, direct the actors, act the leading part, compose the musical scores and be the producer of the film. If anyone can do several jobs, there is no reason to stop him, but genius cannot be the standard in any field.

Usually some co-operation is necessary. Ralph Linton said the best co-operation between two disciplines comes when they are both under the same skull, and there is a good deal to be said in favour of this; but often more than two disciplines are necessary. Two or more individuals may plan a co-ordinated scheme of research. In this way different disciplines can attack a related scope of materials. Conferences of experienced members of selected disciplines can be called to encourage integration of research plans. Such a group can initiate projects and when they are carried out by the individual members, can reconvene to consider the results. A sponsor, either a university, a scholarly association, or a foundation, will probably be needed to give sufficient cohesiveness to insure fruition.

Teams organized on a more formal basis have the advantages and disadvantages of more frequent and intimate interchange of discussion between the researchers. To attain the advantages of teamwork, we could do well to follow the cybernetics model. Norbert Weiner noted that a physiologist with a problem he could not solve that was essentially mathematical could get no help from ten other physiologists who knew no more mathematics than he did; but one mathematician could help him. However, the physiologist has to know enough mathematics to state his problem in mathematical terms, and the mathematician must know sufficient physiology to explain the solution to the physiologist. The two principles are the selection of the team on the basis of the problem, and the furnishing of an elementary training of each member in the basic essentials of the other's vocabulary and concepts.

Many teams, even when qualified in this way, fail to produce results. Very often this is because of the personality factor. The selection of the members of a team should involve a consideration of how well they can work together without conflicts of temperament. This may seem extraneous or an unwarranted mother-hen attitude, but neglect of this factor can bring the teamwork to a halt, the project is uncompleted, and the finances wasted. This may not be the only disadvantage of a team to be guarded against. The frequent interchanges of information from one specialist to another may influence one at mid-point in his research and re-direct his efforts in a new direction. This destroys research designs and interferes with later comparisons. Some degree of isolation may be necessary.

Teams need an institutional home. This may be provided by a university or by an African studies institute within a university. Learned Societies or research-sponsoring foundations may provide the institutional basis to enable a team to undertake its work.

Until the present moment, none of the possible 'angels' has

even considered supporting a multi-disciplinary team on a project of historical reconstruction in Africa or anywhere else. But perhaps this will come about some day.

The highest stage of organization of research of this type is what I would call an Institute of African Historical Research. As I conceive of it, such an institute would have a staff of historians and archivists who worked with written sources, and it would also have archaeologists and anthropologists with various specializations, as well as linguists and selected types of biologists, and a geographer, since mapping of distributions is so important. There would be a place for a few short-term appointments so that whenever a need arose for an unexpected specialization, as in the nature of this kind of research is bound to happen, there would be a possibility of calling in someone until the problem was solved. Essential to such an institute would be a director with the breadth to supervise the numerous facets of the institute's research, to plan the phasing of the work of each discipline concerned in a given project.

The advantage of an institute over a succession of occasional teams is that there would be greater continuity of research. Priority of problems could be established and a long-range plan of research followed. There would also accrue the accumulation of unwritten archives: tape recordings of oral traditions (and their translations); dried and pressed ethno-botanical specimens; photographic files of rock-paintings and the plastic arts, and so on.

We are not likely to see such an institute established in the near future, if at all, because of the many difficulties implicit in the idea; but I am firmly of the opinion that because of the diffuseness of the materials, the analysis of which is necessary to African history, that we will never achieve a deep and broad synthesis of Africa's past until somehow, at some time, an Institute of Historical Research is finally set up.

Co-operation is more effective in the collection of data than in the writing of history. Here, undoubtedly, the individual remains supreme.

No matter whether one works as an isolated individual or in some larger grouping of scholars, there are a number of questions to be answered in the focus of the research. How can we define our project so that the different strategies lead us, as far as possible, to the same spatial and temporal co-ordinates? And who are the people, or the peoples, that we seek to know, to rediscover? The groupings of the past are not those of the present. They are either larger or smaller, they occupied territories with different boundaries and they were composed of ethnicities, some of which have survived and some of which have disappeared. For some purposes, the present boundaries can serve as a guide, and much of the modern historical writing on Africa has in fact managed to keep within these confines; but for many other historical problems the present boundaries are irrelevant and then the spatial and other limits that are pertinent must be determined.

The boundaries of states do not always remain the same; in fact, they tend not to be stable but to expand, contract, fluctuate. If we look at an historical atlas we will see that there was a difference in the expanse of the Roman Empire at the time of Augustus, of Trajan, and of Marcus Aurelius. This may be shown in a series of maps showing the growth and later decline; or on a single map where each acquisition will be marked in a distinctive way, by a special colour, hatching, or individualized boundary. Within the area there will usually be a date indicating the time that Roman administration became effective, and there may be a terminal date to show when the territory was lost to Rome. China under the Han and succeeding dynasties; Muscovy expanding in Europe and then Russia subsequently extending into Asia; stages in the consolidation of the Iberian Peninsula; the growth of the United States of America from the Atlantic to the Pacific; all of these would normally be shown in a way which would represent the diachronic dimension. But when we look at attempts to show African states, there is usually no indication of changes of boundary during the life of the state; we do not find this kind of distinction until the 'partition' of Africa is reached and the distribution of colours on the maps is an overflow from Europe. Most often, in fact, we do not even find boundaries, properly speaking, designated at all. We may find a series of circles with broken lines to inform us that only a schematic outline is attempted. Sometimes when a circle is obviously inadequate, we may find that a segment has been deleted and the area looks like a pie that has been cut and a piece removed, or perhaps the circle projects its arc outwards on one side to include an important town that does not fall within the selected radius from the capital.

At the present time we sometimes cannot do better, but in some cases extant knowledge should give us better cartography if as much concern were put into such maps in Africa as is done elsewhere.

When we lack written records on boundaries, we should look for oral records. If these have been forgotten, we can work, somewhat more tenuously, from archaeology, when we have more exploration of sites. Each state had a cultural identity, and some characteristic artifact can be taken as an index of its presence, but we cannot always distinguish between trade contacts and conquest because conquered peoples would retain much of their original culture. With oral traditions and archaeology together we ought to get reasonably satisfactory results, but with one alone, it would be more tentative.

Whether working from written records (perhaps early explorers' works) or oral traditions, we may have difficulties with identities of ethnic groups. The people that are called Yoruba in the English literature are called Nago in French writings. Fulani and Peul have the same relationship, to which should be added that German writers may call the same people Fulbe. These are now so well known as to cause little trouble, but there are countless ones that are less obvious. We can perhaps best take an example of the complexity of the situation by a European example. The people we call Germans, the French call Allemands, the Italians, Tedeschi, the Russians, Nemetski, the Danes, Tych, and they call themselves Deutsch. A variant of this latter word we use to refer to a neighbouring and related but different people. In addition there are general terms used as synonyms, such as Teutones and (grossly inaccurately), Huns. For earlier historical periods we may use a term like Goths, or a series of names for constituent groups: Marcomanni, Franks, Longobardi, Saxons, Suabians, etc., and there are still regional names, Bavarians, Hessians, and so on. And we ponder whether they are to be included in particular references to Hyperboreans in ancient texts. We have numerous analogues as complex as this in Africa, and it will usually take a good deal more labour to sort them out.

When the human grouping and the extent of its areal occupation have been identified, we would ask, what strategies are called for? The answer is determined by two conditions. First, the availability of data for a particular strategy. If there are no paintings or plastic arts, we can do nothing in the way of art analysis. If a people have given up their own language, as the pygmies have, and adopted another, there is a limitation to what can be done with linguistics. In the most extreme case, where the people are extinct, or their descendants unknown, we would have only archaeology to rely on.

The second factor is resources. The individual searcher can do only as much as his own skills permit; a team can be so organized as to include every skill that is pertinent. The individual needs financial support of some kind—even if he furnishes it himself—and a team becomes an expensive proposition.

In addition to the strategies of the various disciplines, and the comprehensive methodology of historical reconstruction, (which, in part, we have still to construct), there are certain general considerations worthy of mention. We work from the known to the unknown. The more that is known, i.e. the greater the collection of materials in any of the categories previously mentioned, the greater the degree of success we may expect in our exploration of the past. We should start from the best-known areas and block out the regions and periods for which we can establish some kind of surety. Meanwhile the collection of data should go on so that we can subsequently move outward into vaguer regions and periods.

From the known to the unknown implies from the present to the recent past; from the recent past to the more remote past; from the remote past to greater and greater antiquity. The direction of historical research, as Maitland taught us, is backward. We peel off the layers of the past like the layers of an onion. But not all layers of the past are of the same thickness. We do not know beforehand how many there are nor how thick each one will be. The definition of the period must be on the basis of cultural stability; a sharp cultural shift, however effected, defines a change of historical periods.

The spatial analogue of this is to work from known geographical regions into neighbouring parts. From Egypt, from

Mediterranean Africa into the Sahara, the Sudan and the equatorial forestlands ought to prove, in some contexts, to be a continuum. From the Indian Ocean coast inland is still far more obscure, but this too may show some progressions when we know more. In later times, the coasts of Upper and Lower Guinea were the routes of entry of innovations. The limitation of this approach is that it emphasizes cultural borrowing, and other methods must be used in conjunction to recover the essential originality of African cultures, its inventiveness and its adaptibility.

Each people who have a distinct culture and a history require certain terms of nomenclature that are peculiar to them. The historian of Rome must talk about *latifundia* while the historian of Russia speaks of *appanage*. The *agora* is important to Greek history and *druid* to Celtic. It would be possible to find substitutes for these words, but historians have usually preferred to use them with all their particular force.

Early European writers mentioned African kings (and even Dukes, Earls, and other titles) but in colonial times they became, at best, Paramount Chiefs. Historians now are tempted to go back to the use of words like king, kingdom, empire, but reader reaction is sometimes hostile. Should it be king or chief? Perhaps it should be *Omanhene* or *Mwami* or *Oba* or *Kabaka*, but if there are too many the narrative becomes confusing. We need general terms, certainly, but African kings had different attributes from European kings. The consideration of terminology for many positions, things, actions and concepts will occupy us for some time, I fear.

Historical reconstruction requires a certain type of mind. To some extent this may come as a result of training but in part it probably happens that individuals with this kind of mind find their proper *métier*. Without imagination, no one can be a good historian; without control over the imagination one cannot be an historian at all.

It takes imagination to conceive of the possibilities; it takes control to suppress the urge to fictionalize. There is a difference between imagination and credulity. Occam's razor must be ever ready; we should always prefer the simplest explanation until we have evidence that a more complicated explanation is necessary. This is not a field for one who likes the rigid sureties such as are available to the grammarian or the mathematician. One must find one's way through a welter of useless detail that is only seen to be useless *after* analysis. Anderson, talking about his own work, gives us what can well stand as guide for us all:

One begins by making a broad survey of the whole problem in its widest aspects, and then gradually, as he becomes increasingly confident about where the most significant data are to be found, he narrows down his investigations to answer fairly precise questions. . . . One has to look here and there for little vestiges of apparent order and work out experimentally from them, with such techniques as can be devised as one goes along. He gets along best who has a flexible mind, who does not think in hard and fast terms, who is used to searching through apparently chaotic materials for such beginnings of understanding as can be built up in a tentative way.[1]

This poses the intellectual challenge and those with 'flexible' minds will respond. To anyone who knows the thrill of Milton's Conquistador 'upon a peak in Darien', this is an invitation. The tribute of Ortega y Gasset to linguists can apply to all historians of this type: 'los hombres menos despuestos de asustarse de cosa alguna'.[2] The earth's surface is virtually explored; the would-be explorer today has a choice only between contemporary society's social problems and the past which depicts our humanness. The exploration of space, by comparison, is nothing. It is a delusion. Space is sterile; there are no men out there and any who venture out will be pitiable. The old Greek saying is still applicable. Man is the measure of all things. And history is the measure of Man.

The next few decades will see, I am convinced, an efflorescence of multi-disciplinary historical research. This will recover for us much of the human picture and give us an increasing abstraction of historical horizons. The pursuit of the history of Africa will also, however, enrich history itself and when the new methodology has proved itself we will see the historians of Europe scrambling to apply it to areas thought to be fully known but which will in their turn be more amply redrawn. This can be one of Africa's contributions to our emerging world culture; it is an undertaking in which African universities and African scholars should be in the forefront.

EPILOGUE

THESE lectures were primarily directed to those who are doing —or who might do—historical research. If you are committed to traditional research on written sources, it is not suggested that you give it up; it is, on the contrary, essential that all who can do such work should continue; but it is suggested that you amplify your arsenal with some additional techniques. Let us consider an example. You could attempt to write a history of Ashanti in the nineteenth century from written sources alone, but you should know that it will be incomplete. It would be like writing a history of France in the same period with only English sources, for virtually all the documents available to you on Ashanti will have been written by Europeans. If you were an historian of France you would know the language, not only to read the archival materials, but also to read the literature, for you would want to know the profundity of French culture, and you would visit the country. You cannot get the equivalent familiarity with Ashanti culture without learning the language, the proverbs, the traditions, and visiting the towns and villages and talking to the people, the *Ahene*, the *Ahemmaa*, the *Akumfo*, and even the *Ahiani*.

For those who do not do research but who teach history or perhaps merely read history for their own satisfaction of the yen for understanding, these discussions may help them to learn to apply a fair critical judgement to works of this nature. For they are certain to be appearing in increasing numbers, and the teacher especially must know how to evaluate them.

To those for whom this book is intended, no more need be said; they will go on and fill in the inadequacies of my suggestions and work according to a constantly improving methodology to discover the past.

NOTES ON THE ILLUSTRATIONS

The illustrations are contributed by my wife, Marta, who has always been an important support in my professional work. We both feel, like Alice, that a book without pictures, no matter how good it may otherwise be, is somehow incomplete. With two exceptions these represent objects in our collection which we love and hope in this way to share with others who feel as we do about Africa. They are related to the subject matter of the text sometimes in only a symbolic way, and even then in the poetic rather than the scientific range of symbolism.

FRONTISPIECE: cloth appliqué figure, made in a village near Abomey. The lion as an animal of power is often adopted as a royal insignia although perhaps less often in Africa than in Europe and Asia; in Africa the lion has to share this position with the panther, the big cat of the forest, as the lion is that of the grass-lands. Either will do well enough to represent the historian's interest in royal power, so often the thread of any history.

CHAPTER ONE: cloth appliqué figure, same provenience. This fantasized bird possibly represents a *seelenvogel*, but is selected here to emphasize, by its wing in its beak, the self-nourishing aspect of introspection, that indispensable part of any intellectual work.

CHAPTER TWO: carved calabash, Oyo. The beauty wrought on this simple material is a better indication of the pervasiveness of the artistic impulses of the Yoruba than their better known wood-carving. In form it reminds me of the ceramic objects archaeologists love to exhibit among their retrieved artifacts, and so I have used it here.

CHAPTER THREE: Twin figures (Ibeji), Yoruba. These have an interesting place in the religious and artistic life of the people who make them, but I have thought of them here as being in conver-sation, perhaps recounting some of the heritage of the ears.

CHAPTER FOUR: Senufo mask: again the twins, and the two mouths, each with a variation of a pattern within it: the pattern of language.

CHAPTER FIVE: Brass figures, Dahomey. This dancing group in ceremonial costume demonstrates simultaneously several levels of interest to the ethnographer: the activity; the situation in which it occurs; the inner meaning; the style of its representation.

CHAPTER SIX: Rock painting, Sahara (Tschudi, Y., *Peintures Rupestres du Tassili-n-Ajjer*, Neuchatel, 1956, after p. 81, fig. 19). Shows the antiquity of the palm in the Sahara and contradicts Gautier's idea that they were introduced by the cameliers; a neat example of the service of art to historical ethno-botany.

CHAPTER SEVEN: Senufo figure, three feet high. Formerly used in initiation ceremonies of girls in a sacred grove; this is a fine example of African wood-carving.

CHAPTER EIGHT: Gold weight, Ashanti. Illustrates proverb that one doesn't smoke while carrying dynamite. As part of a system of weights and measures, used here to represent chronology.

CHAPTER NINE: *Adikra*, Ashanti patterns carved from gourds to stamp textiles; each has an esoteric meaning. The upper one, called *Obi nka obi* (One person doesn't bite another) enjoins social harmony; the lower is said by J. B. Danquah, (*The Akan Doctrine of God*, London, 1944, p. 93) to represent a war captain. The progress of one form into another is, to me, an illustration of process.

CHAPTER TEN: Incized drawing on a calabash, Bubaque Island, (Bernatzik, H. A., *Im Reich der Bidjogo*, Wein, 1951, p. 193). The intricacy of this line drawing as well as the training and discipline necessary to dancing and its co-ordination to music are comparable to the complexity and permutations of organized research.

NOTES ON QUOTATIONS NOT IN TEXT

FLYLEAF: Collingwood, R. G., *The Idea of History*, Oxford University Press, 1946, p. 238.

HEAD OF CHAPTER ONE: Leopold von Ranke, 'Aufsätze zur eigenen. Lebensgeschichte'in *Sammtliche Werke*, ed. by A. Dove, LIII, 61.

HEAD OF CHAPTER TWO: J. Desmond Clark, *Prehistory of Southern Africa*, Penguin, 1959, p. 36.

HEAD OF CHAPTER THREE: William Shakespeare, *Richard III*, Act III, Scene 1.

HEAD OF CHAPTER FOUR: Antonio Tovar, 'Linguistics and Prehistory' in *Linguistics Today*, ed. by A. Martinet and U. Weinreich, New York, 1954, p. 217.

HEAD OF CHAPTER FIVE: Franz Boas, 'Methods of Cultural Anthropology' in *Race, Language and Culture*, ed. by A. Leser, New York, 1948, p. 276.

HEAD OF CHAPTER SIX: Lewis Carroll.

HEAD OF CHAPTER SEVEN: *Maximen und Reflexionen*, ed. Max Hecker, in *Schriften der Goethe-Gesellschaft*, XXX (1907), 229. Art: another nature, also mysterious, but understandable, for it springs out of the understanding.

HEAD OF CHAPTER EIGHT: Collingwood, op. cit., p. 251.

HEAD OF CHAPTER NINE: Ernst Cassirer, *Essay on Man*, Doubleday Anchor, 1953, p. 225.

HEAD OF CHAPTER TEN: Collingwood, op. cit., p. 247.

NOTES

CHAPTER ONE

[1] *Rats, Lice and History*, New York, 1935.

[2] Louis Gottschalk, 'The Historian and the Historical Document' in Social Science Research Council Bulletin 53, New York, 1945, p. 12.

[3] Loc. cit.

[4] Loc. cit.

[5] James Harvey Robinson, *The New History*, 1913; cf. also H. E. Barnes, *The New History and the Social Sciences*, New York, 1925.

[6] Charles Beard, *An Economic Interpretation of the Constitution.*

[7] Alfred L. Duggan, *The Devil's Brood*, New York, 1957.

[8] See, for example, the Ancient Peoples and Places Series, published by Frederick A. Praeger, New York.

[9] W. E. F. Ward, *A History of the Gold Coast*, 1948.

[10] M. J. Field, *Social Organization of the Ga People*, 1940.

[11] Ms. submitted to the seminar on Ethno-History at Dakar, December 1961, under the auspices of the International African Institute.

[12] R. G. Collingwood, *The Idea of History*, Oxford University Press, 1946, p. 277.

[13] John Martin Vincent, *Historical Research*, New York, 1911, p. 17.

[14] Collingwood, op. cit., p. 276.

[15] Marc Bloch, *The Historian's Craft*, New York, 1953, p. 65.

[16] Ibid., p. 62.

[17] Ibid., pp. 61–62.

[18] Thomas Carlyle, *On Heroes and Hero Worship*. I used the edition prepared by H. S. Murch, New York, 1913.

[19] Georgii Valentinovich Plekhanov, *The Role of the Individual in History*, New York, 1940; *Selected Philosophical Works*, Moscow, n.d.

[20] Max Weber, *The Protestant Ethic and the Spirit of Capitalism*, tr. by T. Parsons, London, 1930.

[21] Emile Durkheim, *The Elementary Forms of the Religious Life*, London, 1915.

[22] T. Parsons, 'Max Weber's Sociological Analysis of Capitalism and Modern Institutions' in H. E. Barnes, *An Introduction to the History of Sociology*, p. 305.

[23] Collingwood, op. cit., p. 215.

[24] Walter Willard Taylor, Jr., *A Study of Archeology*, Menasha, 1948.

[25] Menéndez-Pidal, *Orígenes del Español;* cf. A. Tovar, *Linguistics Today* (ed. by A. Martinet and U. Weinreich), New York, 1954, p. 217.

CHAPTER TWO

[1] W. F. Albright, *The Archaeology of Palestine,* Penguin, 1949, p. 9.

[2] *Geschichte Afrikas,* Köln, 1952.

[3] *The Etruscans,* Pelican, 1955, Ch. 2.

[4] *See* P. Diole, *4,000 years under the Sea,* Pan Books, London, 1954. F. Dumas, *Deep-water Archaeology,* London, 1962.

CHAPTER THREE

[1] W. Grimm, *Kinder-und Hausmärchen,* Leipzig, 1856, III, 427 ff. Translation: Margaret Hunt, *Grimm's Household Tales,* London, 1884, II, 575 ff.

[2] F F Communications, No. 3, Helsinki, 1910.

[3] Cf. 'The Life History of a Folktale,' Ch. V, Part 4, *The Folktale,* by Stith Thompson, New York, 1951, pp. 428–48.

[4] F F Communications, Nos. 106–109, 116, 117, Helsinki, 1932–36.

[5] *Zoölogical Mythology,* I, 30.

[6] *Myth in Primitive Psychology,* 1931.

[7] *La Formation des légendes,* Paris, 1910.

[8] *Africa: Its Peoples and Their Culture History,* New York, 1959.

[9] 'I see no reason at all why the two kinds of study—the historical and the functional—should not be carried on side by side in perfect harmony. . . . I do not think that there are many disadvantages in mixing the two subjects together and confusing them.' *Structure and Function in Primitive Society,* eds. Evans-Pritchard and F. Eggan, Glencoe, The Free Press, 1952, p. 186, n. 1.

[10] *The Greek Myths,* Penguin, 1955, passim.

[11] William R. Bascom, *Journal of American Folklore,* Vol. 67.

[12] B. Malinowski, *Sex and Repression in Savage Society,* London, 1927.

[13] W. A. Lessa, 'Oedipus-Type Tales in Oceania,' *Journal of American Folklore,* LXIX (1956), p. 63.

[14] 'Oral Tradition and History,' *Journal of American Folklore,* XXX (1917), 161–67.

[15] Denys Page, *History and the Homeric Iliad*, University of California Press, 1959.

[16] N. Glueck, 'The Bible as Divining Rod,' *Horizon*, Nov. 1959.

[17] T. D. Niane, *Soundiata*, Présence Africaine, Paris.

[18] A. Kagame, 'La poésie dynastique au Rwanda,' *Mémoires de l'Institut Royal Colonial Belge*, Bruxelles, 1951; cf. *Zaïre*, 1947.

[19] J. Roscoe, *The Baganda*, London, 1911; *The Bakitara*, London, 1923; *The Banyankole*, London, 1923.

  R. Oliver, 'Traditional Histories of Buganda, Bunyoro and Ankole,' *Journal of the Royal African Institute* (1955), LXXXV; and *Man* (1954) LIV; *The Uganda Journal* (1953), XVII; *ibid.* (1959), XXIII.

[20] 'History on the Luapula,' *Rhodes-Livingstone Papers*, 1951.

[21] *De la tradition orale*, Tervuren, 1961. (See my review *American Anthropologist*, 1962); also, *Journal of African History*, Vols. 1 and 2.

[22] Now printed in *Transactions of the Historical Society of Ghana*, Vol. V, Part 1, Legon, 1961.

[23] David Tait, *The Konkomba of Northern Ghana*. Tait's papers were collected and edited by Jack Goody and published by the Oxford University Press, for the International African Institute in 1962.

[24] *The Akan Traditions of Origin*, London, 1952.

[25] See my review, *Journal of American Folklore*, Vol. 72, 1959.

[26] Bk. IV, 154.

[27] *De la tradition orale*.

CHAPTER FOUR

[1] *Time-Perspective in Aboriginal American Culture*, in *Selected Writings of Edward Sapir*, ed. by D. Mandelbaum, University of California Press, 1949.

[2] *Cours de linguistique générale*, Paris, 3rd edition, 1949, p. 118 (translation mine).

[3] *Anthropology Today*, ed. by A. Kroeber, p. 265.

[4] Op. cit., p. 267.

[5] *Linguistics Today*, ed. by A. Martinet and U. Weinreich, New York, 1954, p. 155.

[6] Loc. cit.

[7] *Linguistics Today*, p. 12.

[8] Berlin, 1923.

[9] Op. cit., p. 461.

[10] Rectorial Address, University of Berlin, 1874, 'On the Training of Historians' in *The Varieties of History*, ed. by F. Stern, Meridian Books, p. 193–94.

CHAPTER FIVE

[1] Bk. I, 10; cf. Thucydides, Bk. I, 6, who also contrasts Hellenes and barbarism on attitudes to nudity.
[2] *Man Makes Himself*, Mentor, New York, 1951; *What Happened in History*, Pelican, New York, 1946.
[3] *The Science of Culture*, 1949; *The Evolution of Culture*, 1959.
[4] London, 1915.
[5] In Johnstone, *Indians of Northeastern North America*.
[6] Loc. cit.
[7] Loc. cit.
[8] *The Idea of History*, p. 239.
[9] *Race, Language and Culture*, ed. by A. Leser, New York, 1948, p. 284.
[10] Op. cit., p. 277.
[11] Op. cit., p. 352.
[12] *Social Theory and Social Structure*, Glencoe, 1949.
[13] *Bantu Studies*, 1958.
[14] Loc. cit.

CHAPTER SIX

[1] *Transactions of the Botanical Society*, Vol. 10.
[2] *See* Forde-Johnston, *Neolithic Culture in North Africa*, University of Liverpool Press, 1959.
[3] *The Origin, Variation, Immunity and Breeding of Cultivated Plants*, Chronica Botanica Co., Waltham, Mass., 1951.
[4] Roland Portères, *L'Agronomie Tropicale*, V, 1950.
[5] This qualification was suggested by M. Miracle. Personal communication.
[6] *Die Haustiere*, Leipzig, 1896.
[7] *Agricultural Origins and Dispersals*, New York, 1952.
[8] *Plants, Man, and Life*, Boston, 1952, p. 78. See also, Anderson's paper in *Evolution After Darwin*.
[9] Op. cit., p. 173.
[10] Cf. the article 'Domestication' by M. Herskovitz in the *Encyclopedia of the Social Sciences*.
[11] *Race, Language and Culture*, New York, 1948, p. 171.
[12] Third edition, Oxford University Press, 1957.
[13] Boas, op. cit., p. 173.
[14] Loc. cit.

[15] Franz Weidenreich, *Apes, Giants and Men,* Chicago, 1946.

[16] *The University Lecture,* 1957, Boston University, p. 8.

[17] 'Blood Groups and African Prehistory,' *Actes du Congrès de Préhistoire, 2nd Session,* Alger, p. 307.

[18] *Plants, Man and Life.*

CHAPTER SEVEN

[1] Lord Lugard, *Dual Mandcte in Tropical Africa;* C. G. Seligman, *Races of Africa.*

[2] E. Ellisofen, *The Sculpture of Africa,* p. 57.

[3] See p. 122.

[4] Ibid., p. 27.

[5] Ibid., p. 29.

CHAPTER NINE

[1] Pp. 21–22.

[2] Pp. 24–25.

[3] *A Tropical Dependency,* p. 317.

[4] Balmer, op. cit., p. 29.

[5] Op. cit., p. 30.

[6] Loc. cit.

[7] Loc. cit.

[8] *Races of Africa,* 3rd edition, pp. 85 and 141.

[9] *Theory and Process in History,* University of California Press, 1960, p. 312.

[10] *Politics and Government in Tribal Society.*

CHAPTER TEN

[1] *Plants, Man and Life.*

[2] Quoted by H. Vogt in *Linguistics Today,* p. 254.

BIBLIOGRAPHY

CHAPTER ONE

Books in which historians discuss their métier are numerous; the ones which I found most useful for my purpose here were:

R. G. Collingwood, *The Idea of History*, Oxford University Press, 1946.

Marc Bloch, *The Historian's Craft*, New York, 1953.

Other works which may be pertinent include:

P. Gooch, *History and Historian in the Nineteenth Century*, Boston, 1959.

J. H. Robinson, *The New History*, New York, 1913.

H. E. Barnes, *The New History and the Social Sciences*, New York, 1925.

CHAPTER TWO

Sir Mortimer Wheeler's *Archaeology from the Earth*, Penguin, may easily head the list of handbooks by archaeologists, not only for its detailed, precise and authoritative treatment but because it is easily available in an inexpensive paperback. Among numerous others are A. J. H. Goodwin's *Method in Prehistory*, South African Archaeological Society, 1953, which takes its illustrative material from African excavations; and *Archaeology in the Field*, Phoenix House, London, 1953, by O. G. S. Crawford, the late editor of *Antiquity* and an archaeologist with experience in Africa. G. R. Willey and P. Phillips, *Method and Theory in American Archaeology*, University of Chicago Press, 1958, which, while it deals with New World problems, expresses the experience of archaeologists in situations of greater similarity to Africa than 'Classical' and 'Biblical' archaeology. Another useful handbook is R. J. C. Atkinson, *Field Archaeology*, Methuen, London, 1946.

We cannot list all site reports, but there are several regional surveys. H. Alimen's *Préhistoire de l'Afrique,* Paris, 1955, of which there is an English translation, covers the whole continent for the Stone Ages. There are three Pelican paperbacks which have already appeared and another to come which as a series will give virtually complete coverage for the same period. These are S. Cole, *The Pre-History of East Africa*; J. D. Clark, *The Prehistory of Southern Africa*; C. B. M. McBurney, *The Stone Age of Northen Africa*; and

O. Davies, *West Africa Before the Europeans*, London, 1967. L. S. B. Leakey's *Stone Age Africa*, Oxford, 1936, is now outdated by recent discoveries, but the revised edition of *Adam's Ancestors*, New York, 1960, sets forth Leakey's interpretation of 'The Evolution of Man and His Culture' in Africa in relation to the rest of the world.

Three conferences of the *Congrès Panafricaine de Préhistoire* have resulted in the publication of some of the conference papers.

On the Iron Age, a popular survey is given by B. Davidson, *The Rediscovery of Africa* (American title: *The Lost Cities of Africa*), 1959. An earlier and less extensive survey is D. P. De Pedral's *Archeologie de l'Afrique Noire*, Paris, 1950. The reports of the Conferences on African History and Archaeology, School of Oriental and African Studies, London University, cover this period also. Two chapters of Sir Mortimer Wheeler's *Rome Beyond the Imperial Frontiers* are pertinent.

Journals of interest are *Archaeology, Antiquity, The South African Journal of Science.*

CHAPTER THREE

J. Vansina's *De la tradition orale* is without any doubt the most important work extant on oral traditions. He has also written 'La valeur historique des traditions orales,' *Folia Scientifica Africae Centralis*, 1958, IV, pp. 58–59; 'Recording the oral history of the Bakuba,' *Journal of African History*, vols. 1 and 2.

However, for the treatment of mythology, Vansina must be supplemented and no single treatment known to me is adequate. Suggested reading would include:

L. J. Gray, *The Mythology of All Races*, New York, 1916.

J. E. Harrison, *Prolegomena to the Study of Greek Religion*, Cambridge, 1908.

A. Long, *Myth, Ritual and Religion*, London, 1867.

B. Malinowski, *Magic, Science and Religion*, Boston, 1948.

J. G. Frazer, *The Golden Bough*, New York, 1907–13.

R. Graves, *The White Goddess*, New York, 1948.

J. L. Weston, *From Ritual to Romance*, London, 1920.

The Folktale by Stith Thompson, New York, 1951, is the best survey of the wider field of folklore. The series of F. F. Communications, Helsinki, is the most important collection in this field.

There are several journals that have over the years carried articles on the validity of oral traditions and myth. *The Journal of American Folklore* and *Folk-Lore* are the English-language publications.

CHAPTER FOUR

E. Sapir's *Time-Perspective in Aboriginal American Indian Cultures,*
Ottawa, 1916, reprinted in Mandelbaum, *Selected Writings of
Edward Sapir,* 1949, is still the most extensive and most cogent
discussion of the problem. J. H. Greenberg's 'Historical Linguistics
and Unwritten Languages' in *Anthropology Today,* ed. by A. L.
Kroeber, Chicago, 1953, is another indispensable work.

CHAPTER FIVE

R. Lowie's *History of Ethnological Theory,* New York, 1937,
although it leaves much to be desired, gives a survey of the historical
schools of ethnology.

The Egyptians and the Origins of Civilization is a good example
of Elliott Smith's thinking.

W. Schmidt's *The Culture Historical Method of Ethnology,* tr.
by S. A. Sieber, New York, 1939, gives the only lengthy presentation
in English of the *Kulturkries* position, but see also C. Kluckhohn,
'Some Reflections on the Method and Theory of the Kulturkreis-
lehre,' *American Anthropologist,* 38: 157–96, 1936, and J. Lips,
'Fritz Graebner,' *American Anthropologist,* 37: 320–66, 1935; F.
Graebner, *Methode der Ethnologie,* Heidelberg, 1911.

An American point of view is that of A. L. Kroeber, *Cultural and
Natural Areas of Native North America,* Berkeley, 1939; also
I. Rouse, 'The Strategy of Culture History' in *Anthropology Today,*
1953, ed. by A. L. Kroeber.

CHAPTER SIX

G. P. Murdock's *Africa: Its Peoples and Their Culture History*
called attention to ethno-botany in relation to African history. A
number of people had already investigated various plants or regions
of the continent, e.g.:

R. Portères, *Agronomie Tropicale,* Sept.–Oct., 1950.

J. M. Dalziel, *The Useful Plants of West Tropical Africa,* London,
1937.

F. Irvine, *West African Agriculture,* London, 1944.

J. K. Matheson and E. W. Bovill, *East African Agriculture,*
Oxford, 1950.

Among the more general books, the following are noteworthy:

O. Ames, *Economic Annuals and Human Cultures,* Cambridge,
Mass., 1939.

E. Anderson, *Plants, Man and Life, Boston,* 1952.

I. H. Burkill, *A Dictionary of the Economic Plants of the Malay
Peninsula,* Oxford University Press, 1935.

D. Bois, *Les Plantes alimentaires chez tous les peuples et à travers les âges*, Paris, 4 vols., 1927-37.

R. Cerighelli, *Cultures tropicales*, Paris, 1955.

A. Chevalier, *L'Agriculture coloniale*, Paris, 1942.

W. N. Chute, *The Useful Plants of the World*, New York, 1932.

C. Darwin, *The Variation of Animals and Plants under Domestication*, London, 1905.

A. Guillaumin, *Les Plantes cultivées*, Paris, 1946.

J. Hutchinson and R. Melville, *The Story of Plants and Their Uses to Man*, London, 1948.

A. G. Haudricourt and L. Hedin, *L'Homme et les plantes cultivées*, Paris, 1943.

C. Sauer, *Agricultural Origins and Dispersals*, New York, 1952.

E. Schiemann, *Entstehung der Kulturpflanzen*, Berlin, 1932.

Schultes, *et al.*, *American Ethnobotany*, Waltham, Mass.

M. Van den Abeele, and R. Vandenput, *Les Principales Cultures du Congo Belge*, Bruxelles, 1951.

N. Vavilov, *The Origin, Variation, Immunity and Breeding of Cultivated Plants*, Waltham, Mass., 1951.

J. C. Willis, *A Dictionary of the Flowering Plants and Ferns*, Oxford University Press, 1931.

CHAPTER SEVEN

Most of the thinking in this chapter is my own, and although no doubt influenced at various points by the ideas of others, I am at a loss for references to direct the reader to further reading on the relation of art to history. Archaeologists and anthropologists have sometimes done this in their work, but there seems not to be a discussion of methodology. Art historians in Europe work in a different atmosphere because they draw heavily on literary resources, and a perusal of their works would provide some suggestions. See especially, E. Panofsky, *Studies in Iconology*, New York, 1939.

Works on African art are, however, numerous. These are only a sampling:

E. Elisofen, *The Sculpture of Africa*.

M. J. Herskovitz, *Backgrounds to African Art*, Denver, 1945.

H. Lavachery, *Statuaire de l'Afrique noire*, Neuchâtel, 1954.

H. Lhote, 'Inventaire et références bibliographiques des peintures rupestres de l'Afrique nord-équatorial,' *Actes du Congrès de Prehistoire*, 2nd Session, Alger, 1952.

M. Trowell, *Classical African Sculpture*, London, 1953.

Y. Tschudi, *Peintures rupestres du Tassili-n-Ajjer*, Neuchâtel.

P. Wingart, *The Sculpture of Negro Africa*, New York, 1950.

CHAPTER EIGHT

Zeuner's *Dating the Past* is an indispensable work on the geological methods of dating. Other techniques are discussed by R. F. Heizer, 'Long-range dating in Archeology,' in *Anthropology Today*, 1953.

Glottochronology has a long literature. D. Hymes's 'Lexicostatistics thus far', *Current Anthropology*, will lead the reader to the previous writings. A critical reaction to this technique is given by K. Bergsland, and H. Vogt, 'On the Validity of Glottochronology,' *Current Anthropology*, April 1962.

Other kinds of chronological problems are discussed (usually sketchily) in the literature cited under the other chapters.

CHAPTER NINE

C. H. Cooley, *Social Process*, New York, 1918, was an early investigator of process. Talcott Parsons's *The Structure of Social Action*, Glencoe, 1949, follows through to a larger synthesis which is not, however, beyond controversy.

Chapter Nine and *passim* of A. L. Kroeber's *Anthropology*, New York, 1948, gives an anthropologist's viewpoint; others are S. F. Nadel's *Foundations of Social Anthropology*, Glencoe, Ill., 1953, and Godfrey and Monica Wilson's *Analysis of Social Change*, Cambridge, 1954.

F. J. Teggart, *Theory and Processes of History*, University of California Press, 1960, and the works of Collingwood and Bloch mentioned in Chapter One provide examples of the thinking of some historians.

BIBLIOGRAPHIC ESSAY ON PUBLICATIONS
SINCE 1964

At the time of my first conceptualization of this book there was no work in existence which covered as wide a range of sources of evidence for historical reconstruction. My focus was on Africa but the methods, of course, could be applied anywhere where data of the relevant categories existed.

Recently, Professor Bruce Trigger of McGill University has brought out *Beyond History: The Methods of Prehistory* (1968). His discussion is more general in regard to area (he has worked on both Iroquois and Nubian prehistory), but the case study he presents is in the Nile Valley. There is much in common between this book and Trigger's, but each is worked out somewhat differently. Whereas *Africa in Time-Perspective* is an attempt to encourage history students to try new approaches, Trigger, writing mainly for anthropologists, assumes the commitment of his readers to the subject and emphasizes the limitations of the available methods. Readers of this book would therefore do well to read *Beyond History* as a "corrective" for my enthusiasm.

While Trigger is the only other author to essay a comprehensive exposition, a volume of conference papers edited by Creighton Gabel and Norman R. Bennett entitled *Reconstructing African Culture History* (1967) presents the methods recommended by two archaeologists, two botanists, a linguist, an ethnomusicologist, an art historian, a physical anthropologist, and cultural and social anthropologists. This book is not to be neglected by anyone interested in the use of unwritten sources in historical reconstruction.

Oral Traditions (1965), an English translation of Jan Vansina's epoch-making study, is a boon to many students in Africa, America, and elsewhere. The experience of those who have followed Vansina's methods indicates the need for flexibility because of the great variation of social structure and attitudes among African peoples. For example, Alan Jacobs working among the Masai showed how effectively the institution of age-grades could serve as a vehicle for the transmission of oral traditions; while on the other hand Dr. Saberwal found the Embu age-grades did not preserve traditions. Vansina meanwhile found out that the Tyo, despite the presence of kingship, did not bother to transmit organized traditions from reign to reign and generation to generation.

Many studies have recently appeared which add significantly to our knowledge of social process and thus furnish us with guide lines in historical reconstruction. *Succession to High Office* (1966), edited by Jack Goody, and particularly the editor's introduction, is indispensable to anyone studying kingship systems. *Population and Political Systems in Tropical Africa* (1968) by Robert F. Stevenson demonstrates the importance of demographic factors in societies. Peter B. Hammond's *Yatenga: Technology in the Culture of a West African Kingdom* (1966) brings to the surface a dimension often neglected (except by archaeologists). A series of works from Victor Turner adds greatly to our appreciation of the social meaning of ritual. Frank Willett's *Ife and the History of West African Sculpture* (1968) is a milestone in African art history.

Collections of useful data are also accumulating. Charts to date eclipses in Africa have been published in the *Journal of African History*. *Abnormal Haemoglobins* (1967) by Frank Livingstone has made serological data available in print.

A most welcome publication is *Zande Trickster* (1967) by E. E. Evans-Pritchard, a collection of Zande folk-tales without the apology that often accompanies such volumes when an anthropologist bothers to publish these less "serious" by-products of his field work. Evans-Pritchard humbly does "penance" for having neglected these materials for so long. One can only hope that this time, as so often in the past, the stance taken by Evans-Pritchard will become a trend among anthropologists. Efforts to organize the published folk-tales and to provide a motif-index for Africa are under way under the direction of Daniel Crowley.

Geoffrey Parrender's little volume *African Mythology* (1968) does not sufficiently address itself to the problems of history. Meanwhile, anthropologists and historians continue to use loosely the term "myth" to characterize those parts of oral tradition which they judge to be unreliable. This usage seems to me unfortunate, for it is inaccurate and will be confusing when studies of African myths are undertaken seriously on a large scale. It would be better to use "fable" to make such a distinction; "fable" has been used in this way at least since the seventeenth century, when Sébastian Le Nain de Tillemont so employed it (*Mémoirs pour servir à l'histoire écclesiastique,* I, XIV-XV). Or the word, 'legend,' which in popular usages connotes a contradistinction to 'history,' could be used. But 'myth' should be reserved for myth.

An indication of the increasing involvement of anthropologists in historical studies is *West African Kingdoms in the 19th Century* (1967) edited by D. C. Forde and P. Kaberry. All of the contributors to this historical study are social anthropologists, and it is a valuable addition to our knowledge whether one reaches it as an historian or as an anthropologist. In the same vein is *History and Social Anthropology* (1968) edited by I. M. Lewis, in which most of the contributors are concerned with Africa, the rest with Europe. The introduction of the editor, however, reveals the intellectual strain which the accommodation of a time dimension causes for some social anthropologists. Cultural anthropologists, never having relinquished diachronic studies, seem more at ease with such problems—though they have interested themselves in Africa less frequently. Africanists, however, can benefit from the conceptualizations of these studies which most often focus on Amerindian cultures. One must give priority of place to the late A. L. Kroeber, who devoted most of his life to diachronic studies. The posthumously published *An Anthropologist Looks at History* (1963), edited by Theodora Kroeber, has the broadest of perspectives. Two *Festschrift* volumes are thoroughly historical: *American Historical Anthropology* (1968), edited by C. L. Riley and W. W. Taylor, and *Culture in History* (1960), edited by S. Diamond. Survey volumes such as *Horizons of Anthropology* (1964), edited by Sol Tax, and *Theory in Anthropology* (1968), edited by R. O. Manners and D. Kaplan, give considerable space and prominence to diachronic studies.

An indication of the increased productiveness in African historical writing is the creation of new journals. *African Historical Studies* under the editorship of Norman Bennett (Boston University) has taken its place alongside *The Journal of African History* as a general continent-wide forum, while the number of local journals in Africa has increased. Other journals are now open to African historical writing. A notable example is *Ethnohistory,* which is published by the American Society for Ethnohistory. In 1966 the name was changed by a vote of the membership from the Society for American Ethnohistory, and the change signified an invitation to scholars of

Oceanian, Asian, and African history to join and contribute. Its members are anthropologists (including archaeologists and linguists) and historians. This is a forum favorable to the testing of concepts and methodology cross-culturally.

This is far from being a complete list of the advances made in the field discussed in this book since the first edition, but it indicates the activity in the varied aspects of historical research.

D. F. McCall

INDEX